Walk with Jesus and you will never be alone!

Michelle Johnson

Walking the Way of the Cross for Caregivers

D1270723

*How to Cope Practically,
Emotionally, and Spiritually
When a Loved One Has a Serious Illness*

By Michelle Laque Johnson

Maria Teresa Publishers
1430 Gadsden Highway, Suite 116,
Birmingham, AL 35235
www.CaregiversOfTheCross.com

Maria Teresa Publications

Cover Image THE BIBLE ©2013 LightWorkers Media, LLC
Courtesy of MGM Media Licensing
Cover Image photographed by Joe Alblas
Cover Design ©2022 Christina M. Walsh
Book Layout ©2022 Elizabeth Racine
Layout Graphics courtesy of Vecteezy.com

Walking the Way of the Cross for Caregivers: How to Cope Practically, Spiritu-ally, and Emotionally When a Loved One Has a Serious Illness / Michelle Laque Johnson—1st ed.

ISBN 979-8-9864914-0-0

Advance Praise for
Walking the Way of the Cross for Caregivers

✝

"This is a beautiful and edifying story of deep faith and good humor, of both Stu and Michelle, in the midst of a great and long-lasting trial. It is full of funny, sad, even tear-causing stories, as well as a great deal of helpful spiritual and material advice. Worth reading."
—*Colin Donovan*, **EWTN Vice President of Theology**

"In this touching and necessary book, Michelle Johnson shares personal lessons learned during her own experiences as a caregiver for her husband. This is a must read for anyone whose loved one has been diagnosed with a serious illness, anyone jolted by a health crisis. Michelle Johnson reminds us that even in the maelstrom of crisis, hope, joy and God's touch are still within reach."
— *Raymond Arroyo, New York Times* **Bestselling Author of** *Mother Angelica, The Spider Who Saved Christmas*, **EWTN News Managing Editor, Fox News Contributor**

"...This book will be enormously helpful to anyone with a sick loved one. It offers invaluable spiritual and practical advice on how to make it through what can be unbearably difficult circumstances. A real godsend."
— *Anthony DeStefano*, **Bestselling Author of over 20 Christian books for adults and children**

"Whether it's a frightening diagnosis of a loved one, or an aging parent that is slowly slipping away, the Simons of Cyrene, are carrying heavy crosses. These are burdens, however, that can and will be lightened as well as enlightened while traveling their own special *Via Dolorosa* alongside Jesus and the Blessed Mother. As someone who journeyed step by step with her husband during his battle with terminal illness, Michelle Johnson knows the ups, downs, twists, and turns the way of the cross may bring. Her pilgrimage provides important spiritual insights and inspirations along with some extremely practical steps that can help us understand more deeply the meaning and the value of suffering. Since no one gets out of this life unscathed, and many of us may be or could be facing similar circumstances someday, this book is a real gift."
— *Teresa Tomeo*, **Catholic Talk Show Host of "Catholic Connection" and EWTN's "The Catholic View for Women" and Award-winning Author and Speaker**

"After having personally been a caregiver for several immediate family members who were terminally ill, I only wish I had Michelle Johnson's book at that time to go through those difficult years of caring for them at home. Besides the physical and emotional strain put on a caregiver, it is the spiritual aspect that is most needed, as Michelle beautifully shares in this book. She gives timeless tips in all aspects of caregiving, and also helps caregivers embrace their suffering cross by walking side-by-side, not only with their loved one, but together with Jesus through the Way of the Cross. I have never seen another book quite like this. Caregivers from all walks of life can benefit from this book."
— *Janet Morana*, **Executive Director, Priests for Life, Co-Founder, Silent No More Awareness Campaign, Author of *Shockwaves* and *Recall Abortion***

"This story is a life journey like no other! It is an incredible love story told through the eyes of the precious caregiver. This story creates true meaning and understanding of caregiving. I

grew spiritually while reading each chapter, so much so, that I didn't want the story to end. It is almost inevitable that we will be faced with loved ones getting sick, suffering and possibly dying. I wish I had read this story 11 years ago when I first became a caregiver. I would have approached things so differently had I known of all the graces and blessings that were all around me."
— *Debbie Georgianni M.A.,* **Author, Speaker, Certified Life/ Wellness Coach, and Co-host of EWTN's "Take 2 with Jerry and Debbie"**

"Michelle Johnson beautifully bares her soul in her new book about what were the most painful and difficult years of her life and does so with a rare generosity of spirit. She tells all — the ugliness of the disease, the complexity and brokenness of the healthcare system, the inner conflicts that tore at her faith and trust in God, the slow breaking of her heart as she watched her beloved husband and best friend die. Alongside these poignant details, she offers solid guidance about everything from how to choose the right doctors and treatments to how to deal with your own — and your loved one's — out-of-control emotions. And all of it is done while faithfully, doggedly, following the Master on His long journey to Calvary. Being a personal friend and co-worker of Michelle, I walked with her during parts of this journey and yet never knew some of the details she shares in this book. Perhaps I didn't need to know them the way the readers who reach for this book will want to do, people who will feel in this text a kindred spirit who offers them not just consolation and empathy, but guidance, hope and, ultimately, the promise that life does indeed go on, albeit in a new and much different way. It took much courage and love of neighbor to write this book, and I pray the Lord will bless every person who has the privilege of reading it."
— *Live Catholic Co-Founder Susan Brinkmann, OCDS,* **"Women of Grace" (TV), Living His Life Abundantly (Radio), Award winning author of *The Catholic Guide to Mindfulness* and 10 other books)**

Dedication

To the bravest, most loving man I have ever known, my husband, Stu Johnson, and to all the thousands of unsung heroes who love and care for someone who is seriously ill. Despite being fatigued and overwhelmed, they demonstrate every day that they know the value of their loved one's life. God will reward their selflessness.

Table of Contents

Jesus Meets the Women of Jerusalem

Jesus is Stripped of His Garments

Jesus is Nailed to the Cross

Jesus Dies on the Cross

Jesus is Taken Down from the Cross and Laid in the Tomb

Resurrection

Epilogue

Appendix

Foreword

Your life is rolling along and all of a sudden a serious medical diagnosis comes in for your loved one or friend. You realize rather quickly that you will be the one entering into the role of a primary caregiver. Now your life shifts in a way you never expected. You are not prepared for this new assignment. You are not even sure you have the bandwidth to handle such a task. But, because of your love and dedication to the person in need, you immediately jump into action.

Here is where the problem comes in. You are doing what you can day after day, without thinking much about the future. Sometimes the person survives and lives, and sometimes you take the person through all the stages to death. More often than we'd like, it is to death. Sad ending for such a noble task. You pour your heart and soul into that special person to the point of exhaustion and illness yourself.

This is what happened to me being the caregiver for my dad for two years and for my mom for 11 years. I suffered greatly – mentally, physically and even spiritually. I was feeling alone, wiped out, and not even sure I did things well for my mother and father. It was a roller coaster ride with a sad ending, death.

I so wish I had Michelle and Stu's story to read before I entered into my new role as a caregiver. It is more than a love story. This book is an inspirational manual of sorts for all approaching and working through a caregiving scenario. Michelle and Stu's journey assists in a multitude of ways. Because Michelle put down on paper the day-to-day journey of their lives, I was able to relate to so many of the details. The tears, the frustration, the laughter, the God moments....it goes on and on. If this story were available to me back in the day, I would have saved myself years of guilt and frustration, which ultimately took a toll on me. I am so grateful that this story is published and now accessible to all.

This story is a true gift for all who read it. You don't have to currently be in a caregiving position to read this great love story. I can assure you that someday you will probably be faced with a situation with a loved one that is overwhelming and out of your skill set. This story reads so beautifully, and nothing is held back. You will forever have a new understanding about love, commitment, and faith during a major life situation of sickness, suffering, and death.

Please read this book over and over again, then share it with everyone you care about. Difficult life situations can become easier when you know others have been through similar circumstances and managed to emerge stronger, wiser, and with a renewed faith.

Debbie Georgianni M.A.
Author, Speaker, Certified Life/Wellness Coach, and Co-host of EWTN's "Take 2 with Jerry and Debbie"

Walking the Way of the Cross for Caregivers

How to Cope Practically,
Emotionally, and Spiritually
When a Loved One Has a Serious Illness

✝ Preface

If you've picked up this book, chances are good that someone you love is seriously ill – and you have been thrust into the role of a caregiver. Like most caregivers, you probably feel scared, anxious, and maybe even a little (or a lot) out of control. You may feel hopeless or determined to fight – or a mixture of both. Many of you will find yourselves having to make decisions about experimental therapies which could prolong your loved one's life, or prematurely end it. You must put one foot in front of the other, even as you constantly question whether you are taking the right step.

I know, because I've been there. My husband endured three separate bouts of cancer over eight years. In addition to multiple surgeries, chemotherapy, and various experimental therapies, he ultimately had his leg amputated up to the hip, and in the final months of his life, he became a quadriplegic. For all but the very end, when I had some in-home help because I couldn't lift him, I was his sole caregiver even as I held down a full-time job.

How to Use this Book

This book is written in the hope of helping other caregivers whose loved ones have been diagnosed with potentially fatal illnesses. You can read it straight through, but the chapters are titled so you can skip to whatever challenge you are facing that day. In each chapter, I use examples from my own experience, which I hope will provide you with helpful guidance, perspective, and prayer.

However, you can also skip to "Lessons Learned" to find quick suggestions about ways to cope with a particular situation. If you need help praying, or just some inspiration and comfort, I begin each chapter with a Scripture verse and end with a prayer. I've also included Reflection Questions to help you think through the lessons contained in each chapter.

The chapters are also grouped under a Station of the Cross, which helps you see how Jesus' embracing of the Cross and walk to Calvary compares with your own. In the Appendix, there is also a section entitled, "Thirteen Saints to Walk With in Hard Times." There, you can find a saint to pray to whose life story corresponds in some way with the chapters you are about to read.

Before we get started, however, I'd like to take a moment to discuss what has become the elephant in the room.

Why the Battle is Worth Fighting

Two kinds of people are likely to pick up this book. The first, and hopefully the largest, group will be those of you whose loved one is ill and who are seeking advice, reassurance, and a companion to accompany you on the journey to which you have been called.

If I had written this book only a few years ago, it never would have occurred to me to write to the second group. However, with the very public suicide of a young girl named Brittany Maynard, and the pro-euthanasia/assisted suicide movement, all of that changed. Some of you may have picked up this book because you, like Maynard and her family, are wondering how there could be any blessings in terminal illness and whether "pulling the plug" (either literally or figuratively) isn't a better option.

I hope to speak to both groups.

As every caregiver knows – or will soon know – the battle is not just fought by the one with the disease, but by the caregiver, and, if you're fortunate, by your entire family. Some of you may be wondering how there could be any blessings in terminal illness. I hope this book will help you find them.

It is also my hope that our story will help you understand why adopting the so-called "death with dignity" viewpoint is more than just wrong – it's a tragedy built on a mountain of monstrous lies. There are millions of reasons to be unhappy, millions of terrible circumstances. I once worked for a man whose wife divorced him and then managed to take away custody of their only son. He lost hope and attempted suicide. Fortunately, he failed.

After his return to the office, the two of us had to go to an unemployment compensation hearing. I was driving and, at one point, I made a turn that he considered to be unsafe. I well remember him hanging on to his seat and shouting, "Are you trying to kill us?!"

He obviously didn't see the irony in his statement – and I did not point it out – although, inwardly, I was smiling, because I could see that, although his circumstances hadn't changed, his hope had been restored!

At some point in our lives, most of us are going to face a set of serious circumstances. There may very well come a day when you ask yourself: What's the POINT? But as this story illustrates, in the blink of an eye, circumstances can change, a new therapy can be developed, attitudes can shift, miracles can and do happen.

Of course, you may say, this man's pain was psychological. If the doctors tell you you're going to die, there's no hope, right? Consider the widely publicized story of Brittany Maynard, a young woman who was diagnosed with a terminal illness at the age of 29. She moved to Oregon, a right-to-die state, with her husband and mother, in order to kill herself. Her battle was so public that that she became the face of the "death with dignity" movement.

If you followed this at the time, you may know that there was another woman, who had been diagnosed years earlier with the same illness. She wrote a public letter to this young woman in which she begged her not to kill herself. She told her that she too had been given a death sentence, but she did not die.

As I will remind you many times throughout this book: Doctors are not God. They are often wrong. But even if you DO die, as was the case with my husband, do you have any idea of the wonderful things that are possible in the months or years that you still have left? Even when you are very ill, good things can and do happen, as my husband and I learned. If Brittany had not killed herself, she would have had time to create more memories with her family – and trust me, unlike the naysayers who will contend that they would all be terrible, I can tell you from experience, many of those memories would have been a precious gift; the gift of a lifetime.

Brittany would have had more time to grow as a human being, which means to grow in love – and to allow her family to grow in love. I want you to know that I learned more about love during my husband's long illness than I learned in the entire 35 years we were married.

Because my husband's first bout with cancer – a very deadly melanoma -- was misdiagnosed for a year – a year! – it was off the charts in terms of size. Melanoma is the deadliest form of cancer. It's a miracle my husband didn't die before we finally got the correct diagnosis.

What if my husband had decided to kill himself once he was told how deadly his cancer was? At one point, a doctor at M.D. Anderson in Houston, Texas, expressed his shock that my husband was still alive. Yet he was able to keep up the fight for eight years.

In today's world, the question is: Why should anyone put themselves through this? Why not just end it all? I hope to answer that by taking you inside our fight for my husband's life. I'm going to try very hard not to preach to you. Like Jimmy Stewart in "A Wonderful Life," I want you to see what *wouldn't* have happened if my husband had taken his own life. I want to show you what "death with dignity" REALLY looks like – and it's not taking a pill to end it all.

Yes, I have a point of view, but I promise that I am NOT going to sugarcoat any of the immense pain and suffering we endured – and yes, I say *"we"* endured because, as I said earlier, when a loved one has a serious illness like cancer, your life – like theirs – is forever changed.

No, our battle, like any real battle, wasn't pretty. However, I do hope to show you that it WAS worthwhile and that, while we would ultimately lose the fight for his earthly life, the more important victory would be ours.

So, let's get started…

STATION OF THE CROSS:
Jesus Meets His Mother

I'm going to start with the Station: Jesus Meets His Mother, because as you will learn in a moment, it was Mary who almost literally took my husband and me by the hand and brought us to her Son Jesus. One of the most encouraging things that happened to Jesus during His walk to Calvary had to be the meeting with His mother, and she is there to encourage us too. While seeing her Son in such a condition undoubtedly broke Our Lady's heart, Jesus' own heart must have lifted at the sight of the woman whose love had supported Him throughout his 33-year journey to Calvary. As caregivers, we are an important source of strength for our loved ones who are traversing their own roads to Calvary. We are other Mary's. Fortunately, neither we as caregivers nor our loved ones who are now patients have to walk alone. Mary, our mother and the mother of Jesus, is there to strengthen us, her children, just as she strengthened her Son. It was the Blessed Mother who brought Stu and me to Jesus, and who stood by us in our trial. She is ready to do the same for you. All you have to do is ask.

Introduction

Our Story in Brief and What to Do First

"Come and hear, all you who fear God,
and I will tell what he has done for me."
PS 66:16 (RSVCE)

A Labor of Love

This book has taken me eight years to write. I would write various chapters and then stop. I would get sick, or I would get overwhelmed, or I just plain couldn't figure out a structure on which to hang our story. Then, on a Good Friday seven years after my husband died, I went to the Stations of the Cross at my church. As we read the various stations aloud, I found myself tearing up and flashing back to scenes from my caregiving days, and I remembered that walking through that experience was, in a very real way, walking with Jesus on His road to Calvary.

But Calvary is all about sorrow and pain, right? Yes, it is about sorrow and pain, but that's not all. Jesus went through his suffering and death for a purpose: our salvation. So, despite the pain, He longed to suffer and die for us; in fact, He found joy in suffering for us. What we often don't realize is that when we unite our suffering with that of Christ's – when we make up in our own bodies what is lacking in the suffering of Christ – there will be joy for us, too.

And not just some sort of supernatural mystical joy – although that will certainly be there. But God Himself is never closer to us than when we are suffering, and wherever He is, joy follows. You can't imagine how much closer my husband and I became as we worked together to try to save his life. It's an experience I wouldn't trade for the world.

Of course, if I had known what was going to happen, I would undoubtedly have run screaming from the room. But thankfully, our story unfolded little by little. Actually, the preparation began years before my husband's illness in a small hamlet in Croatia, called Medjugorje. As many now know, the Blessed Mother is reported to have appeared there. I want to state upfront that I will, in obedience, bow to any decision that the Church makes about the apparitions. As St. Teresa of Avila said, "I am a daughter of the Church!"

But whatever the decision, I can tell you that something profound happened to us in Medjugorje. I share the story now because our conversion was the key to our handling the suffering that would eventually come our way. I also want to acknowledge that it was Mary who took my husband and me by the hand and led us to her Son Jesus, and that it was Jesus who was the rock upon which we built our house.

I was a Cafeteria Catholic

It may be hard for people who know me now to believe, but even though I had a wonderful Catholic upbringing, I ended up going to a very progressive "Catholic" college. My family had moved to Spain during my high school years, so when it came time to go to college, I opted to go to my mother's alma mater in Baltimore. I had family there. I knew if I needed help, I wouldn't be alone.

Unfortunately, my mother's college had changed drastically since she had graduated. At the time I attended, we were given no real religious formation. The "religion" books they had us read were all about some amorphous being called God who was sort of "out there." It's a miracle I kept my faith.

There was no teaching about the immorality of abortion. In fact, I remember telling my mother that we didn't have to believe what the Pope said about contraception because he didn't deliver his pronouncement from the Chair of Peter. Where in the world did my 18-year-old self get that? I certainly didn't know anything about the Chair of Peter.

During my time there, I was also taught about the women's movement with no Catholic filter. Equal Rights was all I heard – and that made all the sense in the world to me! I resolved to have a career. I didn't want to have to depend on a man. What if he left me with a bunch of kids? How would I support myself? I wanted to be in control.

Fortunately, all of this didn't stop me from meeting and marrying the love of my life, Stuart "Stu" Johnson, a truly great man. He was not only smart, he was an athlete who was an All-State football player in high school. Although he went to the Naval Academy to play football, he quickly decided that the sport he most enjoyed was rugby. In fact, he frequently came to pick me up for a date with a fat lip or a black eye. He also loved sailing.

But I could not have cared less about his athletic prowess! That had nothing to do with why I fell in love with him. As I said to my mother before we married: "He makes me laugh; he can admit when he's wrong, and he's always willing to try new things." Those traits turned out to be the key to a happy marriage – at least for me!

Stu, of course, went into the Navy upon graduation from the Naval Academy. After 10 years, he left the Service and went into specialty gas sales, a job that took him around the world. He stayed there until his conversion, which I will talk about in a minute.

My first job was as a Personnel Assistant for a large hotel chain. After 10 years of climbing the corporate ladder, I left to get a master's degree in Journalism from Northwestern University in Chicago, and I worked at a number of newspapers, including a regional newspaper, a national newspaper, and a trade journal.

I loved being married to Stu. He called himself a "Northern Baptist," meaning there was none of that charismatic singing and shouting, but he didn't go to church. I decided that if I was going to call myself a Catholic, I should go weekly, so, except for Christmas and Easter when Stu came with me, I went to church by myself. I prayed, but mostly when I wanted something. I prayed that God would bless MY decisions. I didn't really know any other way.

The only time my husband ever got angry at me over my faith was after his mother died. His mother was cremated, and her ashes scattered. There was no service.

I said to Stu, "You know, we really should pray for your Mom."

He got indignant. "Look," he said, "I know you believe in that purgatory stuff, but I don't. My mother suffered from cancer for years. She's in heaven."

I threw up my hands in mock surrender. "Okay, sorry."

We went along like this for years, just enjoying life, working, traveling, and dreaming about the future, but our faith lives, such as they were, were separate.

One day, a package arrived from my sister Marian. It was a stack of books about a place called Medjugorje in Croatia. I had heard that Our Lady was appearing there to six children, but I really didn't know much more about it.

My sister knew I was a voracious reader, but at the time I was busy, so I put the books aside. One day, I picked one up out of curiosity – and, after that, nothing was ever the same. I believed what I was reading, probably because what I was reading reinforced all I had been taught growing up. It's just that now Our Lady was saying it! I felt like St. Paul when he was struck off his horse.

Overnight, I started going to daily Mass, praying the Rosary, fasting, and going to confession weekly. I cried – a lot – but they were tears of joy because I knew – to use a Protestant expression – that I was being saved.

My husband, meanwhile, was observing all of this and wondering what was happening with his wife. Fortunately, this man truly loved me. He listened, he learned, and one day he said: "Do you want to go to Medjugorje?" Did I? Of course, I did!

"Then, we'll go," he said.

"*WE'LL* go?"

Years later, I asked Stu why he wanted to go with me on that fateful trip. He said it was because he knew something important was happening to me, and he wanted to be part of it. He didn't want me to change without him. Such a good man. Our Lady would honor that big time!

Conversion

As we were getting on the plane to begin the first leg of our trip to Croatia, I said to my husband: "You know, there will probably be a lot of praying there."

He laughed. "I notice you waited until we got on the plane to tell me that!" But then he added, "Honey, I know that. I brought along some hiking boots. I'll be fine." Little did he know.

The first night we were there, just before Mass at St. James Church, I showed Stu how to say a Rosary. The next night, I was saying my own prayers when I happened to glance over at my husband. He was crying. My husband was kind of a macho guy. He didn't cry.

I looked away and kept praying. I looked back. Now, he was a complete mess. I looked over at him and mouthed, "Do you want to go outside?" He nodded.

As we sat on a bench outside the Church, I asked what him had happened. I can tell you now, if I would have had to guess what he was about to say, we'd still be sitting there. This man, this Protestant, looked at me and said, "There is a purgatory – and my mother is there."

To say I was flabbergasted is an understatement. In my head, I was saying to the Blessed Mother, "What are you doing?!!!" To him, I said: "How…how do you know?"

He said while he was sitting in the Church, he was holding photos in his hands of people our friends had asked us to pray for. He had his eyes closed. All of a sudden, he felt like someone came up behind him and took him by the shoulders and he felt something like electricity running up and down his arms. He opened his eyes to see who it was and what was happening, but no one was there.

Instead, he suddenly had this crushing sense of – he didn't know how to describe it – not really despair? sadness? – in his chest – and he was just given to know that this was how his mother was feeling.

"Okay," I said, desperately trying to make everything right. "It's okay. Your mother isn't in hell. She's in purgatory. That's where most of us go. We'll talk to a priest."

A short time later, the priest we spoke to told us: "This is a great grace. Your mother needs prayers."

As you can imagine, she got them! However, my husband made me promise I wouldn't tell anyone in our tour group – yes, we were on a tour – that this had happened to him. He didn't want them to think he was crazy.

We were in Medjugorje several days when Stu walked up to me and said yet another thing I never expected to hear from him: "If I was wrong about purgatory, what else have I been wrong about? I want to become a Catholic." I was stunned, but I also realized Our Lady knew what she was doing, even if I didn't!

Stu would indeed become a Catholic, and we would return to Medjugorje the following year so that he could receive Communion in St. James Church.

Even as Stu became a Catholic, I was becoming a secular Carmelite. In case that's a new term for you, you should know that every religious order in the Catholic Church has a secular arm. In the case of the Carmelite order, there is a seven-year formation program for the laity. Lay people who join these orders really are members of the order, even though they may be, and often are, married.

Among other things, secular Carmelites promise that each day they will pray at least 30 minutes; recite morning and evening prayer from the Liturgy of the Hours (the prayer of the Catholic Church, which is said around the world at every hour of every day); spend 15 minutes doing spiritual reading, attend daily Mass as often as possible, and have a devotion to Our Lady, which for most of us means praying at least one Rosary. There's more, but that gives you an idea of the seriousness of this commitment. Little did I know what a lifeline this would prove to be.

After my conversion, I left secular journalism for religious journalism and eventually went into communications.

Stu's path was very different. He graduated from the U.S. Naval Academy, which requires graduates to give back at least five years of service to the Navy. Stu had to stay in slightly longer because he hurt his knee playing rugby and was not allowed to be discharged until he was fully rehabilitated. He probably spent about a decade traveling the world selling specialty gases for a Fortune 500 company, before deciding that the toll on his health was not worth it. To my surprise, he said he had always secretly wanted to teach high school physics! So, he took classes to get credentialed and was thrilled to get a job teaching physics at a comprehensive vocational technical school, where he changed many students' lives.

There was, for example, the student whose uncle was training him to be a drug dealer. (Yes, seriously.) My husband helped him get a summer internship at a large manufacturing company, which changed his life. As a former Naval officer, Stu also acted as the liaison between recruiting officers and his students. Before signing their enlistment papers, he helped these teenagers understand that they needed to negotiate for assignments in which they would learn the skills they would need should they later decide to return to civilian life. He also helped them understand that some jobs – such as flying a helicopter – were a lot more dangerous than others so they should think twice before signing up for them. He also helped students in, say, the automotive track understand that if they wanted job security and top pay, they should learn how things worked and not just what buttons to push on a machine to get their jobs done.

Stu also insisted that his students learn to think and not just memorize facts. He fought against failing students being "socially promoted" so they could stay with their friends. Here's an example of why that was important. In one case, the administration changed the failing grade of one of his students so he could graduate and go to art school. My husband predicted the boy, whom he was working with, would not last because he didn't have the study skills he needed to do well. Sure enough, the student flunked out in the first semester. This upset my husband because he thought the boy could have been spared this fate if he had been kept in high school and teachers like himself had continued to work with him.

Stu was making such a difference I thought the Lord would want him to continue with a job that my husband clearly saw as a vocation. But the Lord had other plans for him and for me –"plans for welfare and not for evil" (Jeremiah 29:11) – just as He does for you.

So, please turn the page and let's begin our journey into the world of terminal illness and caregiving.

PRAYER:

Mary, our mother, please bless everyone who reads this book, and help them to feel, in a tangible way, the tenderness of your motherly love for them. Help them to turn to you when things get hard. If you were willing to ask your Son to help the couple at the Wedding Feast of Cana, just to prevent them from being embarrassed, how much more you will be willing to help your children when they are suffering. We know you are the shortcut to your Son Jesus, who never refuses you anything. Please protect us now, give us a small portion of your faith and the "fiat" of your own life so that this trial may bring us closer to you and to your Divine Son. Amen.

STATION OF THE CROSS:
Jesus is Condemned to Death

Our Lord and Savior Jesus Christ was condemned to death by Pontius Pilate. Today, it's doctors who usually deliver a potential death sentence – it's cancer, it's ALS, it's congestive heart failure – and then they give patients (and their caregivers) an idea of how long they can expect to live. While we appreciate what doctors do, we must remember that they are not God. He alone brings us into being and He alone should decide when we die. As we take our journey to Calvary, our job is to fix our eyes on the God-Man who embraced His cross with courage and who continued to reach out to His disciples, Mary His Mother, Veronica, Simon, and the holy women of Jerusalem even as He was fulfilling His destiny. Before He died, Jesus fulfilled every one of the Father's plans for our salvation. Rest assured that just as our Father had a plan for Jesus, He has a plan for you and your loved one. Ask for the grace you need to trust Him – and be not afraid.

Chapter 1

It's Serious!

"God is our refuge and strength, a very present help in trouble.
Therefore, we will not fear though the earth should change,
though the mountains shake in the heart of the sea;
though its waters roar and foam,
though the mountains tremble with its tumult."
- Psalm 46: 1-3 (RSVCE)

Everyone who gets a serious diagnosis has their own story.

My husband's story began with an annoying little "bone bruise" on the heel of his foot, the size of a pin. He put a tiny bandage on it.

It grew a little larger – to maybe the size of a quarter. He mentioned it to a doctor he was seeing for a completely different problem. The doctor shrugged it off.

It continued to grow. Now we were both concerned.

What neither of us realized at the time is that doctors often don't see beyond the "obvious." My husband Stu had always been fearless. As a child, his mother said she was constantly taking him to the emergency room because he would leap off the top of stairs like Superman and throw himself into or over any obstacle in his path. He had been an all-state football player in high school; played rugby at the U.S. Naval Academy; spent hours participating in triathlons when we were first married; and literally lifted a refrigerator during one of our many military moves. In fact, my mother used to say that he was the kind of guy you would most want to have with you if you ever found yourself alone in a dark alley.

Unfortunately, this "man's man" had gained a significant amount of weight over the years because of back and knee problems caused by all of his "full-on" athletic pursuits. Doctors no longer saw him as a physical specimen, but as one overweight man.

"You have a non-healing, ulcerated pressure wound," they told him at the wound care clinics of not one, not two, but three of the top hospitals in Pennsylvania. "Stay off of it." He was given a cane, then placed in a walking cast, and later relegated to a wheelchair.

Months passed. The wound grew.

Why wasn't it healing?

Lesson Learned: If you aren't getting satisfaction from doctors in one specialty, don't just get a second opinion from another doctor in the same specialty. Find a doctor in a different specialty. This is very important.

One day, my husband was sitting in the office of our chiropractor. He asked my husband how things were going with the "wound problem." A nurse sitting in the reception area happened to hear Stu's tale of woe. She told him he needed to see a team of doctors she knew at an urban hospital in downtown Trenton, New Jersey. Desperate, my husband got their number and made the appointment.

"How old are you?" asked one of the doctors when my husband arrived at their offices.

"Fifty," my husband said, "and I've been dealing with this for a year."

"You're too young for this," the doctor replied. "We'll operate on you and clean this up."

They scheduled my husband for an operation the following week. We were thrilled. Finally, someone was taking action. Life was good. My husband would get well. That weekend, we scoped out the location of the hospital in which they would operate that Monday. To me, the building seemed kind of seedy. Not like the "better" hospitals we had visited in the past. However, my husband liked the doctors, so we decided it would be okay.

The day of the operation, I dropped my husband off at the hospital. Unlike the other operations my husband had undergone, I didn't stay for this one. I had a big day at work and this wasn't really an operation; just a "minor procedure" – a "debriding" they called it. Basically, they would clean off all the dead skin and find the good skin underneath. After being freed from all the dead skin on top, the wound would have a chance to really heal. No big deal. I planned to pick my husband up later in the day.

However, during the debriding, as a matter of routine, these doctors did the one thing that no one at the "better" hospitals had bothered to do. They biopsied the wound – and that made all the difference.

The phone rang at work. My husband said he was ready to be picked up.

"How'd it go, hon?" I asked cheerily, expecting to hear only good things.

Instead, my husband said the two words that changed everything.

"It's cancer."

The bottom dropped out of my world.

Lesson Learned: If your loved one is sick and no one seems to be able to figure out why, consider that it might be cancer or some other major illness. Make an appointment with an oncologist; that is, a cancer doctor, or with a doctor in another specialty. Even if it turns out not to be cancer, you will have eliminated a leading cause of death from the roster of possibilities.

I was so shocked that, instead of leaving immediately, I took the microwave lunch I had brought to the office, went into the break room and microwaved it. It wasn't until I returned to my office, sat down, and raised a fork to my mouth that I came to my senses. What was I doing? I got up, said a quick goodbye to those who needed to know, and cried all the way to the hospital. To me, a diagnosis of cancer meant my husband was going to die – soon.

However, I wanted to be strong for Stu, so, I pulled myself together and managed to get to the hospital just as the doctors entered his hospital room. (Thank you, God!) My husband looked as grim as I'd ever seen him. I stood next to him, and took his hand. He squeezed – hard.

The doctors told us that Stu had melanoma. Huge. Fast-growing. Deadly. We needed to find a cancer doctor. This wasn't their specialty.

But it was Friday afternoon and no doctor's offices would be open until Monday.

We had a little more than two days. Two days to pore over the Internet and get panicked, or, I should say, even *more* panicked. Two days before we could begin to find help. Two days before we could even begin making sense of what was happening.

Two days to turn to God. *Why, God? Why?*

How could this be? We had been to the top hospitals in Pennsylvania. In fact, at one point, I heard a voice in my head tell me: "If you don't pay attention to this, you will be sorry." So, I had called in a favor from a friend whose husband was on the board of one of these hospitals. A doctor at that hospital had seen my husband right away. Unfortunately, every doctor Stu saw was a "wound care specialist." These doctors saw only what they were trained to see; not what was actually there.

Lesson Learned: Don't rely on the reputation of the big hospitals. That is no guarantee you will get a doctor who cares enough to look beyond the "obvious." In our case, all they saw was one big man who "obviously" just needed to lose weight.

Lesson Learned: Cancer – and other diseases – often don't act the way they are "supposed" to act. Stu's melanoma started on the bottom of his foot, and it grew from the inside out! But, you may say, isn't melanoma a skin cancer? That's not always the case; in fact, as we discovered, it's often not the case. If you have a wound that won't heal, get it biopsied as soon as possible.

REFLECTION QUESTIONS:

- What are you doing – or what could you be doing – to better cope with your shock and fear at this diagnosis?

- Is the possibility that your loved one may die impacting your faith? If so, who might you ask to help you better handle this spiritual crisis?

PRAYER:

Dear Jesus, You foresaw what would happen to You in the Garden of Gethsemane and, in your fear, you sweated tears of blood. However, fear did not keep You from doing what You needed to do for love of us. Like you, we're scared...so scared. However, unlike You, our path forward isn't clear to us. Please grant us the wisdom to see what we need to do in this moment; the fortitude to follow through; and the love we are going to need to support each other throughout this journey. We also ask for the grace to stay in the present moment, which is where You are; to turn our backs on all the "what if's" that might happen to us in the future. Help us to know – with all that is in us – that just as the Father was with you on Calvary, You are with us now, our God, our strength – a very present help in time of trouble. Amen.

Our Lady of Good Health,
pray for us.

Chapter 2

Panic – and Regaining Control of Your Emotions

"I sought the Lord, and He answered me and
delivered me from all my fears."
- Psalm 34:4 (RSVCE)

To say my husband and I were in shock over the initial diagnosis doesn't even begin to describe our feelings. Cancer had never entered our minds. I immediately got on the computer to try to make sense of what we had been told. But instead of giving me hope, those searches made me feel that the situation was even more desperate than I had feared.

> **Lesson Learned:** Until you have talked to a least a few doctors and have some idea of what you are really facing, try to stay off the computer. You want to feel better, but chances are, you will feel worse. Instead, focus on the Lord. The rest will come in due time.

My normally decisive husband was paralyzed with fear, and I was so scared I couldn't eat or sleep. Then, I had an extraordinary experience that changed everything. At the time this happened, I was working as the Editor-in-Chief of *The Catholic Standard & Times*, the newspaper for the Archdiocese of Philadelphia. I had been writing a weekly column for several years, but it was getting near to Christmas, and I had no idea what to say.

I asked my Managing Editor to find a column written by someone else. She said she couldn't. I told her to try again. She came back with the same answer. Finally, after three tries, I decided I had no choice but to write SOMETHING. I closed my office door and the following column literally poured out of me. I have never believed I wrote this on my own. I know it was the Holy Spirit who wrote it through me. Here is what I wrote, in real time:

EMMANUEL: WHEN YOUR LOVED ONE IS SERIOUSLY ILL

By Michelle Laque Johnson

(Reprinted with permission. *The Catholic Standard & Times*, December 2005, p. 2)

On Aug. 12, 2005, my husband of almost 29 years was diagnosed with cancer.

The horror of that diagnosis was compounded by the fact that the cancer – a particularly virulent form of melanoma – had gone untreated for a year.

It began as a sore on the heel of his foot. He went to five different doctors, including a highly regarded local wound care center. All misdiagnosed the cancer. They said he had a "non-healing ulcerated wound," a pressure wound. Their advice? Stay off your foot.

They gave him special shoes, a cane, a wheelchair. He started to have trouble getting up in the morning due to extreme fatigue.

In July, I began a novena to Our Lady of Mount Carmel. Shortly thereafter, my husband met a woman who advised him to go to an aggressive team of doctors in Trenton. Within days, they had him in the hospital and were operating on his foot. Only then, only in this non-heralded hospital in the middle of Trenton, was a biopsy taken. That's when they discovered the cancer.

My husband was still in the hospital when the biopsy results came back. He called me at work to tell me the news. A medical oncologist was coming to see him that afternoon.

I left work and cried all the way to the hospital. Until he read this column, my husband didn't know that. Then, I pulled myself together and walked into the hospital room. The oncologist, who had previously worked at Fox Chase Cancer Center, had already arrived.

Here's what we were told. "The cancer is very deep. The cancer is very aggressive. Chances are good we will have to amputate your foot, possibly your leg, up to the knee, so a prosthetic will fit comfortably. Because it has gone untreated for so long, chances are good it has spread. We're sure you will want to go to a hospital nearer to your house, so you are free to go."

As the doctor talked, I reached for my husband's hand. He held on tight. We got his things together and we left. I talked a lot. The doctors aren't God. They don't know. We will find the best doctors. It's not like we live in the country. We live in an area with a lot of good hospitals.

But it was Friday night - and we had an entire weekend before we could make phone calls and try to get any appointments.

We got home and we hung onto each other.

I was terrified. And I was cold, so cold.

"Please God. Please ..."

I could barely move. I had a hard time breathing. My entire body felt as if it had been weighted down. I mechanically went about doing what needed to be done.

Somehow, we got through the weekend. Monday was the Feast of the Assumption, an archdiocesan holiday, so we were able to call doctors' offices all day. It was hard to get appointments. Hard to know the best thing to do. Shouldn't you get a couple of opinions? We called everyone we thought could help, but we didn't get as much done that day as I had hoped. I wondered how I would be able to function at work the next day.

On Monday night, I went to bed. I had been having trouble sleeping, but this night sleep eventually came. At least for a short while.

That night, I remember waking as if from a nightmare to a nightmare as everything came crashing in on me and fear held me prisoner once again.

But in that memorable moment, I breathed what is probably the purest prayer I ever prayed or ever will pray. With every fiber of my being straining toward heaven, I mentally said one word:

"Father!"

And, in that instant, I felt a warm presence, a ball of unbelievable energy, right beside me, leaning against me, and an unspoken question.

And I prayed, "Father, if that is You, come."

And instantly, I was flooded with peace and with – could it be? – joy. My body relaxed, my mind let go of the paralyzing fear. Love had me in His embrace – and I drifted off to sleep.

There's a lot more to tell about this story, and I will tell it in the months to come. I was going to save this story for Lent, when I thought it would be more appropriate. I wanted to write about something more "positive" for Christmas. So, I tried twice to write a column, and nothing came.

On Monday night, I said to the Lord, "My column is not coming together. I guess you don't want me to write this week. The only thing on my heart is the story of my husband's cancer, but I can't write about that at Christmas."

And then, in prayer of course, it came to me. What do you think Christmas is? Christmas is about Emmanuel, which means "God is with us." And that's what this story of cancer is all about.

God is with us not just in good times, but, *most especially,* in bad times. *That* is the Good News.

We read so often about depression and suicide at this time of year because most of us believe that Christmas is supposed to be like a Norman Rockwell painting. We forget that the first Christmas was nothing like that.

Jesus was born to a poverty-stricken couple who were miles from home. There had no friends or relatives to help them. Mary, nine months pregnant, had to ride a donkey. They were rejected, treated like riff-raff. No one would take the couple into their homes. There was no hospital.

Joseph must have been desperate. He finally finds a dirty old stable, filled with animals and straw and he, and an exhausted Mary, who is about to deliver a child, stumble in. It's December and it's very cold. The couple are freezing. There are no blankets or pillows – or running water. The only place to put the child is a container in which the animals eat their food.

That's the real nativity. Yet into that nightmare comes the Son of God – and Mary and Joseph are filled with joy.

God is close to us always – but He is never closer than when we are suffering and in pain.

However, while God is with us, He does not force Himself upon us – ever. Mary had to open herself to God, to say, "fiat," be it done unto me according to Your word – and she had to trust God. Joseph had to do the same.

And so do we. Unlike the hardhearted innkeepers, we have to open the door to our hearts to God – and to His will. There were many times in those first weeks and months after the cancer diagnosis was made that I lost that gift of peace – and, make no mistake, it is not earned, it is pure gift.

I felt like Peter, who was able to walk on water as long as he kept his focus on Christ, but who started to sink when he transferred his focus to his fear of the waves and the impossibility of what he was doing.

The only way I could regain God's peace was by repeatedly saying, "fiat," even when my heart was breaking, and by reminding myself that God is Love and Love always wants what is best for us.

Sometimes, it's not easy. But here's the promise. When you and I invite God in, when we make the decision to trust Him no matter what, when we say, "fiat," even when it's hard, *especially* when it's hard, God comes. And then, no matter what time of year it is, no matter what is happening in our lives, it is always Christmas.

I didn't know it at the time, but in this experience of God's overwhelming Love, God the Father was strengthening me for an eight-year journey into the world of cancer. I pray that anyone who reads this book will know and understand that anything good done by me during this time was done solely and completely through the power and love of God the Father; Jesus, His Son; and the Holy Spirit. I made the decision to be by my husband's side no matter what, but it was God's love and support that made the implementation of this decision possible. I could not have done any of this without His help, without His love – and neither can you.

I pray that you will quickly discover, as my husband and I discovered, that God is faithful; that He does not leave us orphans; that He is indeed "a very present help in trouble" Psalm 46:1 (RSVCE).

Lesson Learned: Make the decision to walk with God throughout this illness. When you lose your peace, renew that commitment. You will never be sorry.

REFLECTION QUESTIONS:

- To bolster your faith and courage, have you and your loved one spent time thinking back over your life together, remembering all the good things God has done for you and the situations from which He has saved you?

- Can you remember a time in your life when God has allowed some suffering which you can now see brought you closer to Him?

- What saints have endured suffering similar to yours? How have they handled it?

PRAYER:

Jesus, to save us from our sins, You were unjustly condemned to die. The human part of You knows very well how we feel about the diagnosis we just received. In the Garden of Gethsemane, you said: "My Father, if it be possible, let this cup pass from me; nevertheless, not as I will, but as thou wilt" Matthew 26:39 (RSVCE).

You wouldn't have said that if the human part of you wasn't scared about what You were facing. We're scared, too. Please give us the grace to say, like you, "Father, if it's possible, please, please, please let this cup pass from us. But not our will, but Thine be done."

Jesus, we trust in You.

**Our Lady, Help of the Sick,
pray for us.**

STATION OF THE CROSS:
Jesus Accepts His Cross

The time came when Jesus had to fulfill His destiny. Even though He had been scourged and crowned with thorns, He now had to pick up His cross and take that first step on the road to Calvary. Jesus knew His path led to certain bodily death. We, too, must take those first steps not knowing for sure what's going to happen. Jesus knew that His journey would save those who accept His Love from their sins and that His steps would ultimately lead to His Resurrection. In our case, we may be given the opportunity to continue our earthly journey or, like Jesus, we may suffer bodily death. But whatever happens, those of us who believe know one thing for sure: Our earthly life is not the end – our hope is in Christ – and that makes all the difference.

Chapter 3

Hanging On to Hope

"They that hope in the Lord will renew their strength;
they will soar on eagles' wings;
They will run and not grow weary, walk and not grow faint."
- Isaiah 40:31 (NABRE)

Most doctors learn in medical school that they should not give you "false hope." In my experience, many of them seem to believe that means they should give you "no hope."

Let me state this unequivocally: DO NOT LET ANYONE TAKE AWAY YOUR HOPE.

"Why?" you may ask. "Isn't that a childish point of view? Aren't you just denying reality?" Here's my one-word answer: "No!" If you have just been medically told to throw in the towel, please allow me to give you some badly needed perspective.

Point #1: Doctors are not God. Not one of them can tell you with any certainty when a person is going to die. My husband's first case of melanoma – on the bottom of his foot – was misdiagnosed for a year. Hear me, a year! It was so large it was off the scale! No one would have given a plugged nickel for his life at the time of diagnosis. But he lived for eight years.

Eight. Years.

In fact, at the point when my husband actually *was* dying and was placed on hospice, I was told he might last a week. But he continued to confound the doctors because the Lord had other plans for him. My Stu lived over a month on hospice until a very special date and time, which the Lord had planned for him and for me, which I will discuss later in this book.

Point #2: None of us knows when a cure for the disease with which you are grappling will be found. It could be tomorrow. That's especially true now that Americans have a "right to try" law, which allows us to take advantage of promising therapies that might otherwise take many years or even decades to be approved. Every day matters. Every day.

Point #3: Far from being foolish, a person who has hope:

- **Seeks alternative cures.** My husband spent hours on the Internet researching such cures, one of which we believe extended his life significantly.

- **Is willing to try experimental medical therapies that could save or extend their life.** It's important to look at the pros and cons of such therapies. Often, the cure is worse than the disease. But sometimes, there is reason to think that this might just work. (See the Chapter on alternative medicine for more on this.)

- **Makes better choices** about what to do with their time thanks to a clearer mind; a mind that is not clouded by the fog of depression, which tells them: "Why bother? It's hopeless."

- **Enjoys a better quality of life.** My husband was always willing to try new things. In the year before he died, we took a vacation to a dude ranch in Wyoming. Really? Yes, really. As my very ill husband said, "I can be sick anywhere!" Big Sky Country was on his bucket list, so off we went. (More on that later, too!)

- **Is more fun for others to be around vs. a patient who is hopeless.** Being surrounded by people who truly enjoy being with your loved one also helps him or her have a better outlook on life.

- **Continues to find a purpose in life.** The last few months of his life, I had to hire in help because my husband had become a quadriplegic and he was too big for me to move myself. I can't tell you the number of these aides who later told me that my husband had made a huge difference in their lives. He listened and provided sage advice to these aides – even in his final days.

Many of you know the story of Our Lady of Fatima, who appeared to three shepherd children in Fatima, Portugal, monthly from May to October, 1917, a little over a year before World War I ended. To prepare the children for these apparitions, an angel appeared to them and taught them this prayer:

"My Jesus, I believe, I adore, I HOPE, and I love You.
And I beg pardon for those who do not believe,
do not adore, do not HOPE, and do not love you."

Why do you think the Angel used the word "hope" in that prayer? One reason is because Jesus is our Hope – our only hope for Eternal Life and for living out the plan for which God created us. We need Him! So, when I say don't let anyone take away your hope, I am also saying don't let anyone take away your God!

Lesson Learned: Choose Hope because Hope is essential. Do NOT let anyone, ANYONE, take it away. Guard it with everything you've got. Your life and the life of your loved one depend on it.

Hope for the Caregiver

The patient isn't the only one who needs to hang on to hope.

I remember one woman in a grief group I attended after my husband died. It was interdenominational because there was no local Catholic grief group. She had been the wife of a pastor, but she was suicidal. The only thing that kept her going was her daughter.

A year or two later, I ran into her. She had regained her will to live. She said her hope had been restored by church members who reached out to her and sent her a Bible, and that had made all the difference. She reflected on her feelings at the time her husband died and said to me: "What kind of faith did I have?" God used her husband's death as a means of bringing her to a more mature and living faith – and now her hope in the future – a future without the earthly presence of her husband – had been restored. Praise the Lord!

At one point, I struggled, too. Catholics, indeed, all Christians, are familiar with the Biblical concepts of faith, hope, and love. Most of us understand the concept of faith, and I thought I understood love (but, oh, how much more I learned about love through my husband's illness). But, at least for me, hope was always a more amorphous concept. I mean who doesn't have hope, right?

Unfortunately not, as I would discover. As we were getting closer to the end of my husband's life, we got to a point where we had seemingly run out of options. We had been to a doctor who pretty much stomped all over my heart. I was sitting in my office, trying to work, but I felt both desperate and defeated. Normally, I could always think of a next step. But this time I couldn't see a way out. I prayed, but at that moment, I was so scared I wasn't aware of receiving any solace.

Normally, I talked to my Mom, who lost my dad in 1989. She's been "there" for me throughout my life, and I don't know what I would have done without her love and support. But this particular day, I didn't want to compound my grief by thinking about my father's death.

I remembered a friend who had more recently lost her husband; a friend who had told me I could call her any time I wanted to talk. Normally, I don't like to "bother" people outside of my family, but for the first time in my life I was desperate enough to reach out for help. So, I got myself together (I thought), picked up the phone, and called Johnnette Benkovic (now Williams).

As soon as she answered, I started to cry. I was horrified, but I couldn't help myself. Because she had been through the death of her own husband, however, Johnnette didn't judge. She didn't tell me to buck up. She just listened. She understood. She shared my pain, and, in that sharing, I felt my hope being restored.

Lesson Learned: When you feel yourself falter, reach out to someone you know who has experienced the same loss you are facing. Talking to someone who understands your pain is a great help. Don't be afraid. This is one of the reasons God gives us the gift of suffering – so we can help others with the wisdom we have been given through our own trials. "Freely you have received; freely give." Matthew 10:8 (RSVCE)

Lesson Learned: Until the good Lord takes you home, you have a purpose. Even if you've never had one before, ask the Lord to help you see it now. There is a reason you are still here. Give caregiving your all. Your rest, your Eternal Rest, will take place on the "other side." You are still in the vineyard. Keep planting!

REFLECTION QUESTIONS:

- Am I demonstrating that I trust God in this situation? If not, what can I do to increase my trust?

- Who do I know and trust that might be helpful in this situation?

- If I am lacking in trusted friends or family, have I asked the Lord to send me someone, trusting that He will answer that prayer? Have I asked the Lord Himself to be that friend?

PRAYER:

My Jesus, I know the road you have specially prepared for me and my loved one is the road to sanctity. No matter how hard it gets, I choose now, with my whole heart, to trust in Your Love and to follow the path You have set before us. When things get difficult, please remind me to say: Dear Jesus, I believe – help my unbelief. Dear Jesus, I hope – help my lack of hope. Dear Jesus, I love – help my lack of love. Amen.

Our Lady of Mount Carmel, Sure Anchor of Hope, pray for us.

Chapter 4

You Can Do This!

"Do you not know that in a race all the runners compete, but only one receives the prize? So run that you may obtain it. Every athlete exercises self-control in all things.
They do it to receive a perishable wreath,
but we an imperishable."
- 1 Corinthians 9:24-25 (RSVCE)

There are going to be times throughout your loved one's illness that are very hard. During Stu's third bout of cancer, I remember standing outside the bedroom where my husband lay waiting for my help. The cancer was rapidly eating up his leg, with open sores that drained foul smelling fluid. My husband needed me to help wrap those sores so they wouldn't drain down his leg and onto everything in its path.

My spirit shrank from the task. Humanly speaking, I did not want to do this. I hesitated outside the bedroom and then spontaneously uttered a short ejaculation that became my signature prayer throughout Stu's illness: "Divine Physician, help me!"

And, in what to me was one of many miracles that occurred during Stu's illness, I IMMEDIATELY received the grace I needed to not only do the task, but to do it with a joyful heart. And yes, I really mean that.

Until a person has faced a serious challenge in life, it's doubtful that he or she has prayed with the fervor one does in a situation that, at least for them, is truly desperate. This is where you learn, if you don't know it already, that God is not some abstract being "out there." He is here and He is listening – to YOU! He cares about YOU! He is ready to help YOU!

But here's the thing: You have to ask.

It begins with a decision. The most important thing you can do is to DECIDE that you are going to be there for your beloved no matter what. No matter what!

But, if you're like me, you then immediately start to worry if you are up to the task. I did. But what I understand more fully now than what I intuitively did then: It's not a matter of gutting it out. In and of myself, I was afraid I wouldn't rise to the challenge. It is only by holding on tightly to God's hand that we are able to stand by a loved one and to do it with love. It's a grace – and that grace is yours for the asking – and it doesn't need to be some long, involved prayer. As I said, mine was only four words.

Divine Physician, help me!

If you are finding it hard to pray right now, please allow me to share this advice from *The Way of Perfection* by St. Teresa of Avila, a doctor of the Catholic Church, who is also known as a master of prayer. She writes:

"The important thing is not to think much, but to love much. … I am not asking you … to make long meditations with your understanding. I am asking you only to look at Him."

Look at Him! Focus your attention on Jesus and on His mother – and ours! – since He gave her to us as she stood at the foot of the cross.

How Will You Choose to Think About this Cross?

Perhaps you are familiar with the book, *Man's Search for Meaning.* It was written by a Jewish psychiatrist named Viktor Frankl, who was imprisoned in a Nazi concentration camp during World War II. It was during that time that he made a discovery that changed his life. He *decided* that the Nazis could take everything away from him, but they couldn't take away how he decided to *think* about it. That one decision saved his life.

What does that tell us as we face an illness that may very well be terminal? In our case, we decided not to accept the doctor's diagnosis that Stu had a short time to live, but to fight. I believe that's why my husband lived eight more years instead of six months.

We also decided not to go it alone. We would walk with Jesus, with Mary, and with some of our favorite saints, including St. Padre Pio, whose bloody glove we were able to touch; St. Peregrine, patron saint of cancer patients; and all my Carmelite friends.

There would be times when Stu would say: "I'm so sorry to put you through this, honey."

But my "Divine Physician, help me" prayer always gave me the grace to respond: "Hey, it's not so bad. We'll do this and then ..." Then, we'll have lunch or take a drive or do *something* fun. I want you to understand, that the ability to do this wasn't wonderful ME. It was wonderful GOD. He's there if we ask Him to be.

The Greatness of Your Calling

In this book, we are going to get down into the weeds of caregiving and talk about all of the hard things. But for this one moment, I want you to come with me to the mountain; to understand the greatness of what you have been called to do.

You have been given the privilege of loving your spouse, your child, your parent, or your sibling through what the world calls the worst of times; the privilege of leading them home to God, to Eternal Life, to a place where people of faith have the hope of being reunited with their loved ones! What could be more important than your loved one's immortal soul? Whether he or she leaves earthly life or lives to fight another day, this experience will change both of you. If you understand your purpose here, it is more likely to make you better rather than bitter.

It is so easy to lose sight of our final end. But once we understand the greatness of our calling, we are much more likely to keep our hand on the plow when the going gets rough. Why? Because we know the truth; we know that no matter what happens, we are not alone. God's Power and Love are never more with us than when we are suffering. He watches everything and waits for us to ask for His help.

We don't always see that the Lord is calling to us during a trial like this. Right now, you are at a crossroads. The Lord waits to see how you will respond. Will you cry out to Him, or will you try to go it alone? Will you choose Love, or will you choose bitterness and resentment? Will you doubt, or will you have faith (and therefore hope) that the Lord will sustain you in this trial? This is a choice, and it's the most important choice you will ever make.

Before you choose, I invite you to consider that this was also the choice of the Apostles, especially our very imperfect first Pope, Peter! He is my favorite apostle because he faltered so many times; yet the Lord made him the rock on which He built His Church.

The story of Peter's walking on water is worth remembering. You will recall that the apostles were out on a lake, far from shore, with waves crashing around them. It was still dark when Jesus appeared to them, walking on water. The others thought he was a ghost. When Jesus told them not to be afraid, Peter said, "Lord if it is you, bid me come to you." And Jesus said, "Come."

So, Peter, the intrepid one, jumps out of the boat into the wind and the rain and huge waves! Imagine watching that! Imagine doing that!

Then what happens? As long as Peter keeps his eyes on Christ, his faith remains strong, he literally walks on water! However, when he takes his eyes off Christ, he starts to sink.

Despite that, he doesn't give up. As he is sinking he says, "Lord, save me!" And Jesus stretches out his hand and lifts him up, saying, "You of little faith. Why did you doubt?"

We are Peter. When we keep our eyes on Christ, anything is possible. Just like Peter, you and I can literally and figuratively walk on water! But when we allow doubts and discouragement to creep in, when we take our eyes off of Christ, we sink. Make the decision now to keep your eyes on the God-Man who suffered and died a horrendous death for you and for those you love. How can you not trust the God-Man who died for you?

Lesson Learned: Call on Our Lord, expect His help, and He WILL give it to you. It really is that simple.

REFLECTION QUESTIONS:

- What are you telling yourself about this illness? Are you telling yourself that it's hopeless, or are you girding yourself for the fight?

- Are you telling yourself that life is over, or are you choosing to see every day as a gift and vowing to live whatever life you have together to the fullest?

- Are you choosing Love, or are you choosing bitterness and resentment?

- How are you showing your loved one that you are in this fight, no matter what?

PRAYER:

For those of you who desperately want to "be there" for your loved one, but who are finding it hard to find the words, please allow me to pray with you now:

Dear Jesus, I want with all my heart to follow Your will, which requires me to accept this cross. I want to be the person my loved one needs me to be. But I know my weakness. I fear that I will not be up to this task. Fortunately, I also know that You are all Powerful, all Good, and all Merciful, and therefore I trust that You will not abandon me. Please, in Your Goodness and Mercy, grant me the gifts, the virtues, the strength that I need to take care of my loved one. Help me to love him (or her) as You love me – perfectly. Amen."

Hold these words close to your heart. Pray them often when the waves start crashing against your boat as they did with St. Peter, and these gifts *will* be yours:

**Our Lady of Consolation,
pray for us.**

STATION OF THE CROSS:
Jesus Falls the First Time…
Simon of Cyrene Helps Jesus Carry His Cross

Jesus fell three times during his Passion, and my husband, like many seriously ill patients, would be felled three times by cancer. As Our Lord's strength started to falter, He needed help to carry the weight of His Cross, so Simon of Cyrene was pressed into service. Cancer – indeed any serious illness – is a heavy cross to bear. Thank you, Lord, for the Simons of this day and time, the good doctors and nurses and all the many healthcare workers who see their jobs as a vocation and who stand ready to help in time of need.

Chapter 5

Assembling Your Team – Doctors

"Have no anxiety about anything, but in everything
by prayer and supplication with thanksgiving
let your requests be made known to God.
And the peace of God, which passes all understanding,
will keep your hearts and your minds in Christ Jesus."
- Phil 4:6-7 (RSVCE)

In the next three chapters, we're going to get very practical. Once you have decided to lean on God, you must set your hand to the plow. Your first task is most likely going to be finding the right doctor or doctors. In our case, and in many others, the doctors who diagnosed the problem were not the specialized doctors we needed; in our case, that was cancer doctors.

Because we faced a long weekend before we could begin calling doctors' offices, I began the process by calling everyone I knew and asking if they happened to know a good cancer doctor. By Monday morning, I was on the phone making the earliest appointments possible.

What I remember most about our first visit to a cancer doctor's office is standing outside the glass door to that office, which was located in a hospital. The reception area was very narrow with the reception desk on the left hand side of the room and a line of chairs on the opposite wall. The chairs were filled with cancer patients. I distinctly remember not wanting to open the door. While I didn't phrase it this way in my mind, I knew I was picking up my cross and, like Jesus, I felt crushed by its weight.

Cancer hospitals are like small cities; everywhere you look there are people fighting for their lives. I knew that once I opened the door our lives would change. This wasn't a war that either my husband or I would have chosen to fight, but cancer had overcome my Stu's immune defenses and I wanted him to live … so I opened the first of many doors – and so will you.

Being diagnosed with a serious illness is scary. Many people think it means they're going to die quickly. If you're afraid of discovering that you or your loved one has something seriously wrong, it's understandable. But you cannot let that fear stop you from going to the doctor. Cancer, like most serious illnesses, is fast moving and waiting is a huge mistake.

During Stu's third bout with cancer, we traveled to MD Anderson where we met a man and his wife who were staying at the same hotel we were. One side of the man's head and face was blown up like a balloon; it was hard not to stare. His wife eventually told us that her husband had refused to see a doctor when he first got symptoms. Now, he was losing both his sight and his hearing. Please…don't wait.

The rest of this chapter will outline nine practical tips that will hopefully aid you in both finding the right doctor and working with doctors in general.

CAREGIVER TIPS

#1: Ask Everyone You Know for a Personal Recommendation

It helps if you can find someone you know who has had experience with a doctor. These recommendations can come from surprising sources. I found the best doctor we had over our eight-year journey through my hairdresser. As she was cutting my hair, I told her about my husband's cancer diagnosis. She told me her mother had died of cancer. I said cynically, "So I guess you don't think much of her doctor."

She stopped cutting my hair and said, "Oh, no, Michelle. I LOVED her doctor. He did everything in the world for her. He even came to her funeral. I can't say enough good things about him." Now that's a recommendation you can trust! As soon as I got home, I called and miraculously got an appointment.

This particular doctor had transferred from a large research hospital to a smaller hospital because he wanted to spend his time with his patients instead of being under pressure to do one more clinical study. While he still did such studies, his patients were his main focus – and that attitude was reflected in the attitude of his staff. This man was so unbelievable that he actually gave us his cell phone number. That's unheard of. We didn't abuse the privilege, but it showed us just how much he cared.

#2: Check Online Reviews, Focusing On Dedication and Care

Even if you get what sounds like a good personal recommendation, cross check the recommendation with other patients' experience by checking websites like www.ratemds.com. I remember getting a recommendation for a specialist at one of the hospitals we were visiting. I checked the doctor's online ratings, which were abysmal. Remember, the person standing in front of you may be best friends with this doctor, or a relative!

#3: Don't be Dazzled by the Hospital's Size or Even its Reputation

As I mentioned previously, it was a small hospital in New Jersey – not the large, prestigious medical centers we visited – where doctors bothered to do a biopsy which showed that Stu's "non-healing ulcerated pressure wound" was really cancer. What's important is finding a medical doctor, regardless of the size of the hospital or its reputation, who takes the time to look into your case; to search for someone who actually cares. Does your doctor or a member of his staff take your phone calls and get back to you promptly with answers to your questions – or are they too "busy" to bother with you?

As we learned, doctors in big hospitals often spend most of their time doing clinical studies, and getting published. They need to find patients who fit a specific profile; patients who are likely to make their statistics look good. (Note: A good result in a clinical trial can mean patients live a few weeks or maybe months longer than predicted.)

These doctors often don't have the time – or care enough – to take on "outliers," such as, in our case, one "big" man, who obviously just needed to lose weight.

During Stu's first bout with cancer, we chose a surgeon from one of the largest hospitals in Pennsylvania, which is where Stu had his first, second, third and fourth surgeries. Why so many?

During Stu's first surgery, the surgeon removed four sentinel nodes. These nodes are the ones that are closest to a tumor so that is where cancer begins to spread. We would soon learn that it's also where lymphatic fluid in the body begins to drain. You will see why that is important in a moment. During the first surgery, the surgeon said he thought he had gotten all of the cancer or what they call "a clean margin." This was great news. Unfortunately, it was also wrong.

When the surgeon discovered that one Stu's sentinel nodes was "hot," he went in a second time and removed seven secondary nodes. When he discovered some of these were cancerous, he went in and removed still more nodes: 26 in all. But that's "only" three surgeries, those of you who are counting may say.

As you can imagine, three surgeries in a short time is quite traumatic and physically hard on a patient. I remember Stu feeling pretty beat up after the third surgery. I spent a lot of time praying with him and calming him down. When I left the hospital that night, my husband was feeling quite peaceful, and I was hopeful he would get a good night's sleep.

Unfortunately, after I left, someone came in to tell him that the surgical team had accidentally left a sponge inside of him and they were going to have to go in again the next day to remove it. That was surgery number four and it occurred at one of the biggest and most prestigious hospital systems in the United States. Big hospitals do not guarantee the best results. They just don't.

#4: With Surgeons, Go for Skill Over Bedside Manner

Unlike medical doctors, patients rarely see surgeons for a long period of time. They operate, do a few follow-ups, and you never see them again. In this case, you generally care more about the skill of the doctor than how friendly they are.

At one time, the husband of one of my two sisters had prostate cancer. I remember my sister and her husband choosing to go with a surgeon who had the bedside manner of a rabid dog vs. a doctor they liked. They made this difficult choice because the former had performed the surgery thousands of times and had a high success rate whereas the latter had performed the surgery many fewer times and had a much lower success rate. Skill is the #1 criteria for surgeons. We'll talk about nurses in the next chapter.

#5: The Friendliness and Efficiency of the Staff is More Important than the Friendliness of the Doctor

When your loved one is suffering from a serious illness, you will most likely have to call the doctor's office at least once after going home. That's why it's so important to pay attention to how the staff treats you when deciding upon a doctor.

In some cases, getting a return phone call can be next to impossible. At one point, I remember deciding the only way to get the answers we needed was to get in the car, drive to the hospital, and stand at the reception desk until the Physician's Assistant finally saw me. I got what we needed! This is why a caregiver is key – and one of many reasons you will learn to be resourceful.

#6: Don't Be Afraid To Do Your Own Research

This tip is for those of you who take in everything the doctor says – and use that as a jumping off point for your own research. That was my brilliant husband. As I mentioned, Stu had a large wound on the bottom of his foot caused by the melanoma. After the four operations above, my husband needed a skin graft. To do this, the surgeon takes a patch of skin from somewhere else on your body (like your thigh) and places it over the wound site. The hope is that this will bind to the wound. After the surgery, Stu's foot was placed in a cast. Stu didn't understand how that was going to work, but the doctor insisted this was the protocol.

However, my skeptical husband, who had a background in physics, didn't just sit around while in a cast that he thought was untenable. He did some research and discovered that bandages impregnated with silver heal wounds much faster than regular bandages. My husband ordered these bandages online and brought them with him to the next appointment where it was discovered that the skin graft had indeed failed. Before the doctor put the second cast on, Stu insisted that this silver-impregnated piece of cloth be placed on the bottom of his heel.

The doctor was not pleased and told Stu that it was "on him" if it didn't work. Stu agreed. Of course, the skin graft was a success. That's why I say, if you are capable of it, consider doing your own research.

#7: Don't Be Afraid to be Demanding When the Situation is Life Threatening

My husband was NOT a hypochondriac, so when he told me he had all the symptoms of a blood clot in his leg (skin swollen, hard, painful, discolored and warm to the touch), I called his primary care doctor, and we rushed over to see her. All we needed was a signed authorization to go to the hospital.

After keeping us waiting for well over an hour in a small, cramped room, a nurse practitioner walked in. "Where's the doctor?" I asked. "Oh, she had a party to go to at her in-laws." I stared at her. I didn't explode, although maybe I should have. I just said, albeit in a quietly furious voice: "My husband has all the symptoms of a blood clot in his leg. Is that, or is that not, life threatening?"

She gulped and looked down.

I remember racing out of that office and going to the hospital, where they immediately confirmed that Stu did indeed have a blood clot. He was quickly admitted. It was the first time I was in the room when they called a Code Blue, meaning he had a heart emergency. It's a wonder he didn't die.

I still kick myself for waiting over an hour to be seen in that primary care doctor's office. I should have demanded we get what we needed immediately. Thank the good Lord, the wait didn't kill him.

#8: Don't Be Afraid to Question Your Doctor(s) or to Get Another Opinion – and to Turn to God When Presented with the "Impossible"

As I mentioned in the Introduction, a number of significant people in my life have had serious illnesses. As I was writing this book, my 92-year-old very healthy, very lucid mother fell and broke her hip. The surgery supposedly went well, but because my Mom kept bleeding, my siblings and I were called into the ICU for a meeting.

When we arrived, three doctors were standing in a semi-circle outside my mother's room, a palliative care person standing beside them. I assume she was there in the event one of us freaked out about what they were about to tell us.

The doctors explained that they needed to go in and do another "procedure" in order to figure out why my mother continued to bleed. However, because of her advanced age, they wanted us to know that they expected her to die on the operating table. Our choice, they said, was either to allow the surgery, or to do nothing and let Mom bleed out.

I thought my younger sister was going to pass out. Having been through several life and death situations, my reaction was quite different. I kept myself from saying, "Seriously?" Instead, I took a deep breath and said, "So the danger in the operation is the anesthesia, right? They agreed. "Okay, we'd like to speak to the anesthesiologist."

My brother nodded. "I think we need to involve Mom in this decision," he said. So, we reconvened around my mother's bed just as the anesthesiologist entered the room.

This was a young hotshot doctor. He looked at us and said, "I don't see what the problem is here. This is a 15-minute procedure. I'll give her the lowest dose of anesthesia possible. She'll be in and out in no time." My siblings and I couldn't believe it!

I turned and looked down at my mother who appeared to be talking to someone. So I asked: "Who are you talking to Mom?" She said, matter-of-factly, "The Blessed Mother."

I was stunned. "What did she say?"

My mother replied, "She told me she would always be with me. Let's go!"

And so, she had the procedure, and she did fine!

#9: Don't Forget to Show Gratitude When the Doctor Does a Great Job

I'm going to have a lot more to say about doctors throughout this book, including a few who made a huge difference in our lives. But here I just want to say that, in a crisis, we can get hyper-focused on the patient and forget to thank those who are helping us. I think I always said the words, but in some cases, I think I could have done a little more – written a note, or, even better, posted a good online review. What does "going above and beyond" look like? Here are a few examples:

- An Alabama doctor who did a number of operations on Stu's leg to remove cancerous lesions in order to make him more comfortable and able to perform basic functions. Eventually, my husband had to have that leg amputated, but this gave him more time to be ambulatory.

- A Florida doctor who spent time with us on the phone answering questions about side effects of a drug Stu was taking even though Stu wasn't his patient. He was an expert on the drug and we had gone to him for a second opinion. We called him when we couldn't get answers from the doctor we were seeing in our hometown.

- The doctor who saw that I, the caregiver, was starting to get sick and gave me some medication because he knew I was too busy caring for my husband to be ill.

- The hospital doctor whose compassion made all the difference as we were preparing for hospice care. That's one of the special doctors I will be talking about in a later chapter.

REFLECTION QUESTIONS:

- Before jumping in and acting like Martha in the Bible, have I spent some time sitting at the Lord's feet like Mary, asking and listening for His guidance as I begin this journey? If not, what's stopping me?

- When action is needed, however, do I step up to the plate like Martha or do I step aside like Mary? How can I find the balance?

- How do I react in life-threatening emergencies? How do I want to react?

- How do I react in non-emergency but serious situations? Again, how do I want to react?

PRAYER:

Dear Jesus, as we begin our journey into the world of hospitals and medicine, please help us to find our Simons; that is, the doctors, and there are many of them, as well as their staff, who will help us carry this cross because they see what they do as a vocation and not just a job. Please give us patience with those who are going to let us down – the patience you showed on the road to Calvary, but also holy boldness when necessary. Most of all, help us remember to offer up our sufferings for those who need our prayers, for those for whom we may have forgotten to pray, and for our fellow patients and caregivers. In Jesus' name we pray. Amen.

**Our Lady of Mount Carmel, Our Aid in Danger,
pray for us.**

STATION OF THE CROSS
Veronica Wipes the Face of Jesus

Jesus was so grateful to Veronica for the kindness she showed in wiping the sweat and blood from his tortured brow that he rewarded her with the famous image of his face. Caregivers are themselves modern day Veronicas. Everything we do with love for those for whom we are caring, we also do for Jesus. Fortunately, as we walk the path to Calvary, Jesus sends us Veronicas in the form of nurses, hospital workers, and home health aides, who wipe our loved one's face, and offer a drink or a supporting shoulder. Caregivers don't always receive thanks for their efforts, but if we do it for God, that doesn't matter. He sees! However, one thing we caregivers can do is thank those who care for us. May our prayers today bless those whom we may have neglected to thank in the midst of a crisis.

Chapter 6

Assembling Your Team – Nurses

*"Trust in the LORD with all your heart, and do not rely on your
own insight. In all your ways acknowledge him,
and he will make straight your paths."*
- Proverbs 3: 5-6 (RSVCE)

Doctors are obviously leading players in a healthcare drama, but
you are going to spend 90% of your time with nurses and other
staff – and hopefully with well-meaning family and friends – so
it's important to talk about all of these players upfront. Their
presence can be your greatest blessing – and, at times, a minefield
– if you're not careful. Let's talk about this.

The Hospital Experience

We discovered the difference between good and bad hospital
care when Stu had the blessing of being admitted to Abington
Memorial Hospital (now known as Jefferson Abington Hospital)
in Lansdale, Pennsylvania, during his second bout of cancer.
While I will deal with this in another chapter, I think it will be
helpful for you to understand upfront the difference between good
and bad care and, most importantly, how to find good care.

Bad or Mediocre Nurses/Hospitals

Nowhere is it more important for a patient to have an advocate – like you, dear caregiver! – than when your loved one is in a bad situation. During Stu's first bout of cancer, we learned to ask for pain medicine well before my husband needed it because it took hours and hours to actually get the drug(s). As you will learn, it's much harder to control pain once it has really taken hold of a patient.

At this same hospital, bed linens and hospital gowns were rarely, if ever, changed – even when they desperately needed to be. I remember wandering the halls of that hospital in search of bed linens and changing the sheets myself!

It was also at this hospital that we discovered that even the floor to which you are admitted can affect the quality of care, so, whether the care you receive is good or bad, remember the floor on which you received it. You just never know when a return trip to that hospital will be needed.

Lesson Learned: If you get good care on one floor, remember that floor so you can request it in the event of a return visit. Obviously, the reverse is also true.

Great Nurses and Other Hospital Workers – and How to Find Them

It was our experience at Abington that showed us it didn't have to be this way. Nurses and Certified Nursing Assistants or Patient Care Assistants at Abington spent time with their patients; they recognized that making them feel like they had a family at the hospital who cared for them truly improved outcomes.

They kept their patients clean – washing them, putting on fresh hospital gowns and changing bed linens as needed. They answered questions and contacted the doctors promptly when that was necessary. They made sure the patients had fresh water, that they got their food, and, most importantly, that they got their medicine, especially pain medicine, in a timely manner.

Why was it so different?

We didn't know it but, at that time, this hospital had received The Magnet Prize for its Daily CARE Plan six years in a row. In fact, this hospital retains that designation even at the date of this writing. That's remarkable because fewer than 10% of hospitals (461 total in 2019) have earned this prestigious prize. You may not be able to find a magnet hospital in your area, but wow, what a difference!

Lesson Learned: If you have to go to the hospital, look for a magnet hospital. You can find one by searching for "magnet hospitals in [YOUR STATE]." It can be a game changer!

Becoming an Effective Patient Advocate

Most doctors have someone, it may be a nurse, or it may be an administrator, who is in charge of getting back to patients who have questions or medical problems after leaving the hospital, and in an emergency. The quality of these people varies greatly. Unfortunately, the friendliness of this person while you are in the doctor's office is no guarantee they will return your call.

Caregivers, you will find that you will, of necessity, get more assertive as time progresses. In one case, I actually had to drive to the hospital, walk in, and wait to speak to the administrator face-to-face in order to get an answer. But in another doctor's office, the doctor himself would call back with needed information.

Here's the dilemma. There is a fine line between being an effective advocate vs. an overly demanding spouse or parent. As caregivers, we have to recognize that this is a stressful time. It's possible that you and I can be wrong.

How do we know? Well, when your loved one is in pain and they are not getting the drugs they need to control it, or when they are sitting in sheets completely soaked with various bodily fluids, you need to take control of the situation.

However, you cannot constantly be ringing for a nurse or a nurse's assistant. These healthcare workers do have other patients, and the administrative demands in most hospitals are onerous. Sometimes, you can take care of a problem yourself, like I did when I found sheets and made my husband's bed. (If anyone had been paying attention, they might have gotten angry, but no one was.)

Other times, patience is needed. It's important to spend time at the beginning of each day, asking the Lord to help you behave the way He wants you to behave. It doesn't mean we will always do the right thing – we are human – but it helps.

Lesson Learned: When you are angry about not getting the answers you need, say a quick prayer – such as "Lord, help me to do the right thing" – before taking action. But please don't be timid about taking action if it is needed. Your loved one is depending on you..

Lesson Learned: It's especially important that your loved one get the pain medicine he or she needs in a timely way. Otherwise, the pain is much harder to control. This is one situation in which you must take charge.

Patient Care Advocates

Most hospitals now employ people known as Patient Care Advocates. These are the people to ask for when you feel that your loved one is truly not getting the care they need or if you need financial, legal, or social support. I had no idea these people existed until late in our healthcare journey.

Well-Meaning Family and Friends

If you are fortunate enough to have family members or even friends who are able and willing to help, that is a Godsend! While Stu and I lived quite a distance from family, they were constantly on the phone and flew down at critical junctures. You want to treat them like the gold they are!

I do want to mention, however, that loved ones can, at times, be overly zealous. In one case, I had a relative whom I absolutely love. She took time out of her busy schedule to help me. However, when she arrived, she had a tendency to figuratively push me out of the way, intervening with doctors and stepping in to take care of my husband. At the time, I didn't want to hurt her feelings because I knew her heart was in the right place. I never said anything because I wasn't quite sure what to say without hurting her feelings.

However, in retrospect, I should have taken her hand in mine and said something like this: "Clare [not her real name], I love you with all my heart, and I appreciate your being here more than I can say. But honey, I need to be the one who talks to the doctors. I need to be the first one to see Stu after a procedure. What I really need you to do while you are here is to support *me*, not *be* me."

I offer you these words in the event you find yourself in a similar situation.

Lesson Learned: Be grateful for well-meaning family and friends, but do your best to *lovingly* let them know when or if they are being a little overzealous.

Medical Receptionists and File Clerks

Every person on the hospital staff is an important part of the success of your healthcare journey, not just the doctors and nurses.

I fondly remember the receptionist who came running out to the elevator after we had left one doctor's office to say: "I'm NOT allowed to tell you if the x-rays look GOOD." And she stared significantly at us. In this case, there was good news, and she didn't want us to go home and worry until we were officially told. How incredibly kind.

I also say a prayer when I remember the file clerk at a Pennsylvania hospital who got me Stu's surgical records in hours instead of weeks so I could expedite the time it took to get Stu into MD Anderson. That's something she definitely did not have to do.

REFLECTION QUESTIONS:

- What is the quality of care being given to my loved one? If it's good, what can I do to show my appreciation? If it's bad, what can I do and who can I speak with to make it right?

- When I'm in a stressful situation, how do I normally react? Is that helping or hurting me in this situation? What can I do to help myself react in a way that will achieve a good outcome for everyone?

PRAYER:

Thank you, Jesus, for the "Veronicas" you are sending my loved one and me on this difficult journey: the nurses, hospital workers, and well-meaning family and friends whose care makes all the difference in the success of a hospital stay. Help me to remember to brighten their days with gratitude when they brighten my loved one's days with their care. At the same time, grant me the wisdom and the courage to speak boldly when my loved one isn't getting the care they need. I ask this of the Father in Your Precious Name. Amen.

Our Lady of Good Counsel,
pray for us.

Chapter 7

Caregiver Toolkit:
Hospital, Pharmacy, Self-Care, and At-Home Medical Savvy

*"Make me to know thy ways, O LORD; teach me thy paths. Lead
me in thy truth, and teach me,
for thou art the God of my salvation."*
– Psalm 25:4-5 (RSVCE)

Before we get any deeper into our story, I want to share a few
things I wish I had known at the start of our journey. Here's how
to set yourself up for success whether you are at the hospital or
at home.

Get Your Loved One's Hospital Records as You Go

Trying to get information from many doctors' offices can be an
exercise in frustration. You can avoid this by asking for your
loved one's records *while you are still in the doctor's office* or as
soon as they are available. In addition, if your loved one has had
an x-ray, a CT-scan, an MRI, or surgery, get the records while you
are in the hospital, if possible, or at least put in a request for them
immediately.

Don't wait until you need them – and you will need them.

You will be meeting many doctors. Here's an example: In the case of cancer, there are surgeons, and there are oncologists who handle the medical side of things. There are different doctors for every type of cancer. An oncologist specializing in melanoma is different than an oncologist specializing in leukemia or breast cancer, and so on. There are doctors who handle radiation, pain doctors, and many more.

When doctors in your geographic area no longer offer hope, many people travel to some of the larger hospitals like MD Anderson at the University of Texas in Houston, which my husband and I credited with performing an unbelievably complicated surgery that extended his life, or the H. Lee Moffitt Cancer Center and Research Institute in Tampa, Florida, which helped us understand that one particular experimental procedure we were considering would not work for us.

Others go to the Mayo Clinic, the Cleveland Clinic, Memorial Sloan Kettering, and more – whatever is closest to them geographically, has doctors with the specialty they need, or offers a clinical trial that may be helpful.

Every single one of these places will need the records of what has happened thus far. You will save yourself a lot of time and mental anguish if you already have them.

Making the Best of Your Loved One's Hospital Stay

When your loved one is in the hospital, you can help them by finding ways to connect them to their "real" lives. My husband was a dog lover. He really suffered when he was unable to spend time with our dog. At one hospital, I was able to wheel him to an outdoor patio on the ground floor of the hospital, then run out to our car, and bring our dog at that time (a Rottweiler named Angel!) over to the patio for a visit. That did more for his mood than anything else could have.

Does your spouse love music? Bring in whatever they need to help them connect to their favorite tunes – an iPhone, a CD player, a radio, a boom box – whatever works for them. If he or she has a roommate, just make sure to bring headphones. Does your loved one like to read but find it hard right now? How about an audio book?

What's their favorite food or treat? In addition to hospital food courts, most hospitals are surrounded by area restaurants. If your loved one isn't on a special diet or fasting for surgery, bring them a treat!

When to Turn to a Hospital Pharmacy vs. a Drug Store

When your loved has cancer or some other major disease, it's doubtful you're going to be able to get the kind of prescription drugs that are required from a drug store. Even if the drug store says they can order those drugs, it's doubtful you will be able to get them in a timely manner. In most cases, your best bet is the hospital pharmacy.

If you're already in the hospital, that's a no brainer, but when the doctor prints out pages of prescriptions for you (yes, pages) while at his office, don't drive around town looking for a pharmacy that can fill it or make dozens of phone calls. You'll save time if you simply drive to the nearest hospital and get them filled.

Organizing Drugs at Home: Set Up a Medicine Closet

The journey of a terminally ill person can be a long one. We got to the point where we had a ton of drugs all over the house. Sometimes, one doctor would put Stu on a drug and then we'd be sent to another specialist who put him on a different set of drugs. So, we had a lot of half-filled prescriptions and creams as well as x-rays from every place we had been.

One day, I was inspired to take over a closet and line it with a couple of small inexpensive bookshelves. I took ALL of Stu's medicines and arranged them so I could find things in an instant. I also piled up his x-rays, MRIs, etc. in one place by date with the most current on top. I called it our medicine closet. Little did I know how handy that would one day become. (See the Chapter on Alternative Medicine for the story.)

If you don't have a closet, find a corner of a room, or a set of cabinets or shelves. If you have young children, just make sure any drugs are above their reach or in a locked closet to which only you have the key.

Finding Joy at Home

As a person gets sicker and their faculties decline, boredom can set in. Here are a few ideas! (See the Resources section at the end of this book for links.)

- **Music:** One thing that rarely fails to cheer up a sick person is music. But it has to be music that your loved one enjoys – and, trust me, that can change radically. My Mom is both legally blind and, at least for now, experiencing some cognitive challenges. When she was healthy, she enjoyed listening to Italian opera singers and really good Catholic music. But at her sickest, she liked military anthems and really upbeat popular music for which my brother made up a playlist. At the moment, she's back to spiritual music, but it no longer has to be sung by Italian tenors! Be prepared for anything!

- **DVDs:** Sometimes a loved one's tastes can be seemingly contradictory. My Mom hates listening to books on tape, but loves listening to Father Timothy Gallagher's EWTN television series, which are available on DVDs. I purchased a really simple portable CD player and DVD player to make these more accessible for her. When my husband became a quadriplegic, I got him a voice-activated device so he could turn on the TV and change channels using his voice.

- **Subscription-Based On-Demand Television:** Many patients, particularly if they are elderly, tend to be very discriminating about the types of TV shows they watch, so, for Catholics, EWTN's On-Demand library, which has both free and rental movies, is a great resource. Many Catholic and Christian film companies also have subscription-based apps, while a subscription to a service like Hulu can be helpful if your loved one prefers older television series.

- **The Great Outdoors:** Sick people don't necessarily need to go to the Grand Canyon or even the local park. Many can find peace and serenity in the back yard. Pick a good spot, a comfortable chair, and bring them a drink and possibly a snack, and many loved ones can be happy outside for some time.

Two Emotional Self-Care Tips

In an earlier chapter, I mentioned that there was a short prayer that made a big difference for me throughout Stu's entire illness. That prayer was: "Divine Physician, help me." In addition to this prayer, there were two other things I repeated to myself on a consistent basis, which got me through some hard times.

- **Breathe:** I can't tell you the number of people I have advised to take a deep, diaphragmatic breath in the middle of an emergency. That's because we tend to breathe shallowly and even to hold our breath when we are stressed. I first noticed this in myself as I left my critically ill husband and was driving in to work. It was quiet in the car, and I just suddenly realized I was holding my breath. So, having been in a choir for most of my youth (my mother was the choir director), I began to consciously breathe deeply through my nose, to hold my breath for a few moments, and then slowly let it out. Try it. I promise, it will do wonders for you.

- **Don't think, just do:** After my husband died, I was cleaning up the office/dining room, and I came across a piece of paper that shocked me. It was a humongous list of all the doctors I had to call and other medical things I had to order or buy or look into that day. If I had stopped to *think* about that list, I would have been overwhelmed. Instead, I well remember saying to myself on a daily basis: "Don't think, just do." That means just what it says. Just plunge in and start making the calls or doing whatever else it is you have to do. While "Divine Physician, help me," was my favorite prayer, "Don't think, just do," was my favorite slogan.

Technology:

One of the things a caregiver often becomes good at is researching options. You may find yourself talking to anyone and everyone about problems encountered because you never know who may know something that will help solve the problem.

While you might expect medical professionals to have some knowledge of how to take care of your loved one once you get him or her home, they often don't. Even if they do, they're unlikely to tell you. Why? Because they're focused on doing exactly what you've hired them to do. You might say: "I'll just ask them about it." The problem is that first-time caregivers usually don't know what they don't know. In other words, you're not likely to ask about something you don't know exists.

So, let's review some of the things that are available and where to find them.

Home Health Care Services:

As we neared the end of our journey, my husband started to lose his mobility. To understand why, we were sent to an outpatient MRI facility. As I paced around the reception area, I came across a brochure for a home healthcare service. At the time, these were

not commonly advertised on television. I didn't even know this existed. Obviously, this costs money, But I was happy to discover there are people you can hire through an agency who will come to your house for as little as four hours a day, one day a week, to perform a variety of duties such as bathing, dressing, and using the toilet; transferring from a bed to a wheelchair and a wheelchair to the toilet; making up a fresh bed with the patient in it, assisting with meals and medication, light housekeeping, and laundry.

I remember taking the brochure and putting it carefully in my purse, so I would remember where it was. My husband was a big man, and I knew I couldn't move him by myself should it become necessary. (It did.) All of this comes in handy if you need to run some errands (like taking the children to school or to baseball practice or going to the grocery store), if you need to go to work, or if you just need a break for a few hours. However, it's important to look at online reviews and to ask your friends if they've had experience with such agencies. The quality varies dramatically.

Medical Aids (Plus How to Make a Bed with Someone in it):

My husband was a big man. Near the end of our journey, he would lose his mobility. I could not move him by myself and, although they said otherwise, neither could some of the home health care aides I needed to keep him at home. At one point, we had a harrowing incident where one of those aides lost her grip on Stu as she was moving him into the bathroom. He was screaming! If I hadn't run in to help, she would have broken his leg.

The next day, a different aide came to the house and said it was too bad we didn't have a Hoyer Lift. A what?

A Hoyer Lift comes with a large heavy-duty canvas-like cloth, which is placed alongside the patient. The caregiver rolls the patient on his or her side, stuffs the canvas underneath them as far as possible, and then turns them over to the other side as far as possible and pulls it out. (Note: This also works when you are making a bed with someone in it.)

However, in the case of the Hoyer Lift, once you've placed the canvas under the patient, you roll the lift over the bed, take the loops on the four corners of the canvas and loop them over the hooks on the lift and then pump the lift with your foot. It slowly raises the person from the bed! You can then roll the lift over to a chair or the toilet, and lower them gently down. The canvas has an appropriately sized hole in the middle to allow a person to go to the bathroom. It's a Godsend.

The aide said that our insurance company would have to authorize it. After the incident with the home health care aide almost breaking Stu's leg, I felt we needed it immediately, and I was concerned about how long insurance authorization might take. So, I went to the Yellow Pages (believe it or not, they still exist, but online obviously works, too!), and discovered I could rent one from a local medical equipment company. Another problem solved.

You may not need a Hoyer Lift, but should you find it hard to do something, you can bet others have, too. Check for technology to solve your problem online. You'll be shocked at what you can find.

Saving Money/Finding Deals

To find out what's available, go to a medical equipment store and just walk around or talk to the sales people. But before you buy or rent something, search for these items online and sign up for catalogs. Almost anything you can find at a hospital is available online. This includes bedside urinals, an overbed or laptop table, grabbers which literally allow you to grab objects while sitting in a wheelchair, and thousands of other items. You can even find walkers that double as seats or that offer places to store items as well as scooters with all sorts of bells and whistles.

I'm discussing products for people with impaired mobility, but you can find catalogs for any kind of disability you can think of. Just go to your favorite search engine and type in catalogs for such things as vision impairment, or hearing loss, or loss of mobility. You will be overwhelmed with choices. You can do the same thing on Amazon.

When I wanted to purchase products for my mother who is legally blind, I went to Amazon, typed in products for "vision impaired" and found an array of magnifiers, talking alarm clocks and bathroom scales, phones and computer keyboards with huge letters and numbers, low-vision playing cards, and hundreds of other items. Once you see what is available, compare prices from different sites.

REFLECTION QUESTIONS:

- What problem is my loved one experiencing which might be solved by technology? Have I done a simple Internet search or asked friends, family, doctors or other healthcare workers for their suggestions?

- What does my loved one like to do that he or she isn't able to do now? Is there something I could get that would allow him or her to do what they love in a new way?

- What sort of spiritual books, prayers, podcasts, TV or radio shows have I found for my loved one so that I'm not just helping them technologically, but spiritually?

PRAYER:

My Jesus, I know that helping my loved one physically is very important, but most important of all is providing them with spiritual support on this road to Calvary. Please lead me to those things that will really help them to find You!

**Our Lady of Mount Carmel,
Dispenser of the Gifts of God,
pray for us.**

Chapter 8

Finding Joy: Maine

*"Teach me, my Jesus, how to maintain joy
in the midst of difficulties..."*

−Mother Angelica

You can find joy, even in circumstances that are not ideal. Let me explain what we faced in the Summer of 2006, and how we still managed to find happiness in the midst of a tough situation.

To summarize, Stu was diagnosed with cancer in August 2005. Over the next six months, he had four operations in which the surgeon removed a total of 26 lymph nodes. After all of these surgeries, the doctor told Stu he had gotten a "clean margin," meaning he didn't think the cancer had traveled anywhere else in my husband's body. Of course, the man had to wear a ski boot with a hole in the bottom to allow the skin graft on the bottom of his heel to "take," and he had to teach the second semester in a wheelchair – but he was alive! How would we celebrate that?

Like millions of other people, Stu and I loved going to the beach in the summer, so that was my first thought. However, when a doctor removes 26 lymph nodes from your body – whether they be from your leg, as was true in my husband's case, or from your arm, as is the case with breast cancer, the affected area will swell up. Our surgeon had told us this MIGHT happen. I still shake my head at this statement. There is no "might" about it. Your body WILL swell. Period. You must take immediate action.

When we finally realized that Stu's swelling was not going to go down, we looked into treatment. Initially, we were told that we had to find someone to perform a special type of massage for lymphedema, as this is called. I watched videos and tried my best to do this type of massage. We even considered traveling to Germany, which is an epicenter of healing for lymphedema.

Fortunately, we discovered that a machine had been invented in the U.S. that massages the leg for you. Five years later, this would make a huge difference for my sister, who was able to use this machine, which had been greatly improved, after she, too, was diagnosed with cancer. Stu wasn't so lucky. His leg and foot never regained their normal proportions.

Because of the lymphedema, Stu's skin started to break down and lymph fluid would ooze out of his pores. That meant we had to wrap his leg from his toes to his groin with compression bandages. Since my husband was always hot to begin with, this was a problem.

Summer was coming, however, and I knew my husband was a big believer in vacations, something my own family had only done sporadically when I was growing up. I also knew he wasn't one to wallow in his physical infirmities, so I was equally sure he wasn't going to let his lymphedema curtail our vacation plans.

Before he could say anything, I started researching alternatives to our standard beach vacation. One of the coolest (literally) places I could think to go in August was Maine. When I told my husband about it, he initially balked.

We would go to the beach because he knew I liked the beach. I was equally adamant. With all that wrapping around his leg, I knew he would be miserable in 80 or 90-degree weather, and walking in sand would be nearly impossible.

It was helpful that I had discovered that Maine is a cool place in more ways than just the weather. Fortunately, I won that battle! Could my sweetheart do everything we would have done if he had been 100 percent well? Of course not. But that didn't stop us from having a great time.

During that vacation, we stayed in a hotel that backed onto a very rocky beach, which is common in Maine. I would walk out early in the morning and sit on a big rock to say my prayers. Then, I would return to the room, and we would get ready to go to breakfast.

On different days, we explored the various towns in the area; we took a wild and windy boat ride in one town and sailed on a catamaran in another. We ate lobster rolls and other incredible Maine seafood. We traveled to Bar Harbor and ate on the deck of a restaurant that overlooked the harbor. We drove through Acadia National Park, stopping to enjoy time at various scenic overlooks.

And, of course, we simply enjoyed being together and away from the hospital. Sure, we had to wrap Stu's leg several times a day, and Stu couldn't walk very far, but that was a small price to pay. It was a great respite and wonderfully relaxing.

Lesson Learned: Your loved one isn't dead. Look for every opportunity you have to celebrate good news – to have some fun.

Lesson Learned: Don't let the perfect be the enemy of the good. Don't look at what your loved one can't do. Look at what they can do and structure your vacation around that. Later in this book, I will give you an idea of what it's like to travel with someone who is truly ill – and why it's worth it if that's what your loved one wants to do.

Lesson Learned: Surgeons know how to repair what is broken or to cut something out of you. We never encountered one that had a clue what to do afterwards. That's why it's so important to talk to people who have had the same illness you do, either in person or in an online chat group. That's how you learn about post-surgical complications and how to deal with them. Don't try to do this alone!

Lesson Learned: In his *Examen* podcast, Fr. Timothy Gallagher teaches us to ask this question: How has God shown His love for me *today*? Any time is the right time to ask this question, but it's never more true than when times are "bad." It's so easy to focus on the negative, especially when your loved one is sick. But he or she is still alive, so you still have the opportunity to create memories. That's just one of your many blessings. Fr. Gallagher says that, for St. Ignatius of Loyola, the worst sin we can commit is ingratitude!

REFLECTION QUESTIONS

- What *specifically* has happened *today,* for which I want to give thanks to God?

- What is my loved one still able to do and what fun times can I structure for us around those abilities?

- What would I have to do – and who might I enlist – to make it possible for my loved one to experience something they have always wanted to do?

PRAYER:

Dear God, as my loved one's illness progresses, help us to look for the joy in everything you are calling us to do. It's always there, just as You are always there, if we will only look. Thank You for helping us discover all the ways You are blessing us during this walk along the Via Dolorosa. Amen.

**Our Lady of Mount Carmel, Our Light in Darkness,
pray for us.**

STATION OF THE CROSS:
Jesus Falls the Second Time

Jesus Himself fell a second time, yet He did not stay down. He knew He had to keep trusting His Father's plan for Him and for the world – and so He staggered on. Throughout any illness, there will be many falls. My loved one was diagnosed with cancer a second time. As his caregiver, I too staggered under the weight of this second diagnosis. Father, help my loved one and me to trust in Your saving plan for us. Like Your Son, Jesus, please help us to get up and soldier on.

Chapter 9

Trust that God Has a Plan,
Even When it Seems Humanly Crazy

"For I know the plans I have for you, says the Lord, plans for welfare and not for evil, to give you a future and a hope."
- Jeremiah 29:11 (RSVCE)

Every so often in a marriage, spouses end up in crisis at the same time. For example, there was a couple we knew at church who had both been diagnosed with cancer at the same time; the wife survived, but the husband did not. Yet the Presence of God was so strong in the wife that after her husband died, she was not destroyed, but was joyful in the Lord. At the time, I didn't really understand that.

In 2007, my husband and I would go through our own double Purgatory: his with his health, mine with a job. During that time, some dear person sent me the Scripture quote above, which sums up what God was doing beneath the chaos.

Stu's Situation

Thanks to Stu's lymphedema, a knee problem he had experienced for years, worsened. By 2007, Stu realized he would have to have his knee replaced. That is a painful operation that requires a great deal of equally painful physical therapy, but we got through it. Although Stu had become increasingly tired, we figured: Who *wouldn't* be tired after all of that? So, Stu returned to teaching, albeit in a wheelchair.

Here's what we didn't know: Once a person is diagnosed with cancer, the likelihood of a reoccurrence ranges from 50% to 100%. I hear you saying: *But surely if you've been through this once, you'd recognize it if it happened again, wouldn't you?*

Actually, no. First, because even the same type of cancer can manifest itself in different ways. However, the primary reason is that there are more than 100 types of cancer, so, while it's possible you might recognize the symptoms of, say, melanoma, that doesn't mean you will recognize the symptoms of leukemia. Feeling tired? Take some vitamins. Eat a little better. Right?

Michelle's Situation: A Testimony to God's Providence

As Stu's fatigue was increasing, but before we realized it was serious, I was invited to a Catholic Leadership Conference, held at the end of October in Charleston, South Carolina, where I spent some time with EWTN's Deacon Bill Steltemeier. We had met many years earlier at the USCCB Conference in Texas, just as the Catholic Church's sex abuse crisis had broken wide open. I had gone to a press conference that had been postponed for an hour or two. Since my hotel was located a taxi ride away, I decided to stay in my seat and organize my notes from the day.

That's what I was doing when, out of the corner of my eye, I saw a distinguished looking elderly gentleman walking down the aisle between the folding chairs set up for the press conference. He got closer and closer to me and then sat two seats down from me. I looked up and smiled.

"Hello."

"Hi," he said. "I'm Deacon Bill from EWTN."

That got my attention! I introduced myself and we began talking. As our conversation wound down, I said to him: "What made you come over to talk to me?" He looked at me and said: "I don't know. You just looked like someone I should know!"

Through the years, I met Deacon Bill at various conferences. At this particular conference, I filled him in on what was happening in my life. He looked me in the eye and said, "We've got to get you down to EWTN."

I looked at him in surprise. "Really?"

He nodded. I honestly didn't know if anything would happen or not, but true to his word, I had a call from EWTN a day or two after returning home from the conference. My husband was thrilled.

I was curious, but a bit skeptical. I loved the idea of EWTN – in fact, I had always had a "feeling" I might work there. But EWTN was in Alabama. It's not that I had a negative impression of the state. I truthfully had no impression! It simply wasn't on my radar, but, as it would soon become clear to me, it was definitely on God's.

EWTN flew me down and put me up in one of a row of guest houses behind the Network. I flew in during the early evening hours. My interview with Michael Warsaw, then Sr. Vice President, now Chairman and CEO, was the following day.

As I was driven past the guard shack, the Stations of the Cross, and the Pieta replica, and into the Network with its giant lighted cross, the driver (an employee) pointed out the famous Chapel of Our Lady of the Angels. He told me it was always open, so that's where I headed as soon as I settled into the guest house to which I had been assigned.

When I walked into the Chapel, all I can tell you is that the Spirit of God rushed upon me. It was so powerful; it almost took my breath away. I sat in a pew for a long time, asking God to bless my interview and to make it clear to me what He wanted me to do. In retrospect, it seems pretty clear, but despite the palpable Presence of God, I was uncertain.

My interview with Michael Warsaw for the Director of Communications position the following morning seemed to go well. He told he would be making a decision soon. I was scheduled to fly back to Pennsylvania later that day, so I returned to the Chapel. Boom! The Holy Spirit hit me again. I returned to the guest house, got my luggage ready to go, and then went to lunch in the EWTN kitchen. Afterward, I stopped by the Chapel. Bam! I kept testing it and, every time I entered the Chapel, God let me know that He was there.

I was a bit early leaving for the airport, so I asked the driver if he would take a little detour around the Network. The homes were beautiful, and, if what he said was accurate, they were quite inexpensive compared to similar homes in Pennsylvania. I was also captivated by the topography. Irondale is in the foothills of the Appalachian Mountains. It's very pretty!

While waiting for the plane at the airport, I called my husband and recounted what had happened. He was certain I was going to get the job.

I remember saying, "But, honey, what about your job?"

He said, "I can get a teaching job anywhere."

"But what about our friends?"

"We'll make new ones."

"But we don't know anything about this area of the country."

"Great, an adventure!"

Obviously, I did get the job. It was probably November or December 2007. Of course, we had to sell our house, and Stu had to finish out the school year. I asked Michael if I could have a little time before starting the job, and he readily agreed. I actually didn't start until March 3, 2008. That willingness to accommodate was yet another sign that this was the right move.

I was very careful to ensure that EWTN's health insurance would cover Stu, since his melanoma was a pre-existing condition.

As I worked to get our house ready to sell, Stu's fatigue was becoming worse. He went to a doctor who said he was anemic. Even before his first bout with cancer, Stu had problems with anemia. He had seen a doctor, who conducted a battery of tests, but the results were inconclusive. This time, however, his numbers got so low that he couldn't make it home from his teaching job without pulling over to the side of the road to take a nap.

This obviously wasn't normal. Because he was anemic, someone recommended he see a hematologist. The week before I was scheduled to fly down to Alabama to start my new job, through the grace of God, I found a good hematologist from, of all people, my hairdresser. During my appointment, I just happened to tell my hairdresser about my husband's cancer diagnosis. She told me her mother had died of cancer. I said cynically, "So, I guess you don't think much of her doctor."

She stopped cutting my hair and said, "Oh, no, Michelle. I LOVED her doctor. He did everything in the world for her. He even came to her funeral. I can't say enough good things about him." Now that's a recommendation you can trust! As soon as I got home, I called and miraculously got an appointment.

This particular doctor had transferred from a large research hospital to a smaller hospital because he wanted to spend his time with his patients instead of being under pressure to do one more clinical study. While he still did such studies, his patients were his main focus – and that attitude was reflected in the attitude of his staff. This man was so unbelievable that he actually gave us his cell phone number. That's unheard of. We didn't abuse the privilege, but it showed us just how much he cared.

I was able to get Stu an appointment for the following week – something that, in our experience, was also unheard of.

The plan was for the two of us to fly back and forth until the school year ended in May. We kissed goodbye, and I took off on my new adventure.

We were trusting that God had a plan!

New Job

The first day at EWTN went well. My husband and I talked and prayed together, and I wished him well at his doctor's appointment the next day.

Day two also went well. I vividly recall the phone call that night. "Hi, honey," I said. "How did your appointment go?"

For the second time in my life, my husband dropped a bomb on me, this time by saying, "I have leukemia."

In the words of the famous Yogi Berra, it was déjà vu all over again. Inwardly, I turned to the Lord. "Jesus, I must have misunderstood what you wanted me to do!"

To Stu, I said: "Honey, I'll quit my job tomorrow and come right home."

He said, very firmly: "No! You are our future. You do whatever is necessary to secure the job."

I remember thinking: "How am I going to do this?" But even as that thought formed, I knew how. *On my knees!*

And so began a real nightmare. During the day, I did my best to impress my new boss. At night, I was on the phone with my critically ill husband who had been admitted to the hospital to begin treatment. I was also on the phone with our real estate agent, trying to sell our home in Pennsylvania. After work, I would sometimes drive around Alabama with Stu on the phone talking about different areas where we might make our new home.

I would leave work on Fridays, drive to the airport, and take a flight to Pennsylvania for the weekend, only to fly back Sunday night to begin work again.

But it was my first visit back to Philly that was the real heartbreaker. The doctor took Stu into the hospital immediately. Unfortunately, the airline I took to Philly, which offered the only direct flight from Birmingham, was almost always late. The first time I returned to Philadelphia, the plane circled the airport for hours; presumably because we left Birmingham so late.

A dear friend of mine, Sue Brinkmann, also circled the airport in her car until that flight landed, then she drove me to the hospital and waited until my visit was over. She was also the friend I called when my husband was first diagnosed with cancer. She listened to me cry on the way to that hospital. How can you thank someone enough for that kind of selflessness?

It was about midnight when we arrived at Abington Hospital. Fortunately, family is allowed in cancer wards any time of the day or night. I remember walking into the room and seeing my husband partially propped up in the hospital bed, sleeping.

I walked over to the bed, gently laid one hand over his, and one on his shoulder, and whispered: "Honey, I'm here."

As I bent over to kiss my husband's forehead, I saw him take in what may have been his first deep breath and let it out in a rush. I wanted to cry. He was obviously so relieved and happy that I was there. We had gone through so much, but we had always gone through it while physically together.

Leaving him to return to Alabama on Sunday afternoon was one of the hardest things I've ever had to do. I asked God if he would allow me to be there for Stu's very first chemo, and, praise the Lord, I was. It was scary to watch what we knew was poison drip from the IV into his veins. The next time I would see my husband, he would have lost all his hair.

My schedule and the emotional toll of my husband's illness was staggering. I remember going to a business conference. I sat down, and someone began speaking. Unfortunately, the person sounded like the adults in a Charlie Brown Christmas Story:

"Wannh wannh waaannh, wannh wannh wannh wannh waaannh."
I dipped my head and tried to concentrate. Why couldn't I hear her correctly?

"Wannh wannh waaannh, wannh wannh wannh wannh waaannh."
I managed to get through the afternoon, but went to bed as soon as I could. When I woke up, I could process things again. But I pray I am never that tired again.

My friend, Sue, visited Stu in the hospital several times while I was in Alabama, and I was thrilled to hear that various faculty members from Stu's school did, too. It turned out the faculty had taken up a collection and bought my husband a laptop computer! In fact, they collected so much money that they gave us the excess, which came in very handy for things like parking and food from the hospital cafeteria.

God's Plan

Eventually, it would become obvious why the Lord had moved us down to Alabama, and if you are in a similar situation, trust that His Plan will become clear for you, too.

Of course, the Lord had a job for me to do, but EWTN is also a place where people walk the talk. The kindness that Michael Warsaw showed to me, as a new employee, still astounds me, and I have seen that kindness extended again and again as Network employees have encountered their own human tragedies.

After the first four weeks or so, Michael allowed me to work on and off from my Philadelphia home. I quickly discovered that EWTN had a cancer rider on its insurance which paid for cancer care from dollar one – no deductible for cancer expenses!

Moving is never easy, but between trying to prove myself at my new job, visiting my critically ill husband in the hospital, packing up our old house, and searching for a new house in Alabama, I was sleep deprived and beyond stressed. In the middle of packing some things up in our old house one weekend, I tripped and fell hard on my knees. I sat there and cried, but quickly realized there was no one physically there to help me. I had to pick myself up off the floor and press on.

As hard as the transition was, however, the Lord constantly showed me He was with me in every way that mattered. My previous job in Philadelphia had taken everything I had. I not only worked late hours during the week, but frequently through the weekend. The commute into the city took at least an hour, more if there were traffic problems, and there were always traffic problems.

I also worked hard at EWTN, but I was able to leave at the end of the day to do what I had to do. When we first arrived in Alabama, we lived in a house owned by EWTN. That house was not only located immediately behind the Network, but was only about 20 minutes from UAB Hospital, where Stu would go for follow-up cancer treatments. Even after we bought a house, my commute would be only 20 minutes because traffic there isn't nearly as bad as it is in Philadelphia, and things simply aren't as far away.

The State of Alabama also proved to be a blessing. The house we eventually purchased cost $100,000 less than our home in Pennsylvania, and was a lot nicer. That money would be very important to us as Stu's cancer journey continued and we would journey out of state for help at MD Anderson in Houston, Texas, and H. Lee Moffitt Cancer Center in Tampa, Florida – and for so many other expenses such as hospital parking, hospital meals, home hospital equipment, ambulances ($600 a pop!) and much more. We also found the cost of living in general, from property taxes to food costs, was much lower.

But what made the biggest difference in Alabama was, and still is, the people. I was surrounded by people who believe. They believe in God; they believe in miracles; they believe in helping each other.

Also, while Alabama is not known as the center of the universe, EWTN is indeed the center of Catholicism in the United States. The incredible people who come to the Network on a daily basis is dazzling. Stu would be prayed over by people like Sister Briege McKenna, and, through EWTN, I would meet the man whose miracle healing was responsible for Cardinal John Henry Newman's canonization, and he would pray over Stu. (More on that later.)

Little by little, we discovered that, even though the road south had been hard, God had truly blessed us with this move. God indeed had a plan for us, and He has one for you too.

REFLECTION QUESTIONS

- How have I shown God – and my loved one – that I truly trust His plan for me in the midst of this illness? If I have not been doing a good job of this, am I willing to stop right now and ask God to grant me this grace?

- If my loved one is not demonstrating trust in God, what can I do to encourage this trust? Can we join hands now and ask the Lord to grant us both the grace to show greater trust?

- What trusted priest, nun, loved one, or person of faith (or even online faith group) might I contact who might be willing to share how they have navigated their own hard times, so I could learn from them?

PRAYER:

"Trust in the Lord with all your heart,
and do not rely on your own insight.
In all your ways acknowledge Him,
and He will make straight your paths."
-Proverbs 3: 5-6 (RSV)

If you start to lose trust in God's plan, think back over your life and remind yourself of the many times the Lord has shown you that something you thought was bad for you was actually for your good. Think about the many times He saved you before you even knew you needed saving. Then, meditate on the Scripture verse above and resolve to trust Him now.

Dear Jesus, how many times in our lives have You shown us that You are there to pick us up when we fall? How many times have You shown us that not only can we rely on You no matter what, but that Your plan is so much better than our own? You trusted in Your Father's plan for You. Who would have imagined that so much good – indeed the Salvation of the World – would come from Your Passion and Death? Help us to trust You as You trusted Your Father, and to love You as much as You love us. Jesus, we trust, help our lack of trust.
Amen

Mary, Mother of Mercy,
pray for us.

Chapter 10

When You Disagree

"But rejoice insofar as you share Christ's sufferings, that you may also rejoice and be glad when his glory is revealed."
- 1 Peter 4:13-14 (RSVCE)

Stu's last chemo in Pennsylvania resulted in a "heart incident," during which he was rushed from the cancer ward in the middle of the night to the cardiac unit, where they proceeded to shock him back to life.

Stu clearly remembered seeing a light at the end of a tunnel and a door that was slowly opening. When he was shocked with those paddles (just like on TV), the door slammed shut. He also remembered being scared he would never see me again; that we wouldn't get to say goodbye. These memories of his broke my heart – and made me thankful he had come to the end of his chemotherapy, or so I thought.

One of the consequences of moving when a loved one is seriously ill is that you need to find a new team of doctors. Fortunately, the Birmingham, Alabama, area has some world class hospitals, including UAB (University of Alabama Birmingham Hospital.) While I no longer remember the exact number of "consolidation" rounds of chemo that the doctor in Pennsylvania wanted Stu to have, I do remember that it was fewer rounds than what the doctors at UAB required.

When You Disagree

I told myself early on in this journey – and I firmly believe this – that even though Stu's decisions radically affected me, it was his life we were dealing with. That's why, in my mind, the patient should always have the final say in his or her treatment. However, when Stu told me he had decided to go for the additional rounds of chemo at UAB, I thought about the heart incident, and I was worried.

I listened to him talk and then said, gently, "Honey, Dr. [Mark] Sundermeyer [our incredibly wonderful Pennsylvania doctor] only wanted you to have two more rounds of chemo. Why do you want to go with UAB's recommendation?"

As always, my husband had a good answer. He said, "Sweetheart, if I don't do this now, and the cancer comes back, I'll always wonder if I could have taken care of it now."

What can you say to that? Unfortunately, the extra rounds of chemo almost killed him but, thankfully, they also killed the leukemia. Stu was officially in remission, but his hemoglobin values remained low.

Lesson Learned: I believe the patient should always have the final say when it comes to his or her treatment. It is, after all, their life. However, we, as caregivers, have the opportunity to act as a sounding board, to help evaluate the pros and cons of a procedure, while always respecting our loved one's choice.

When Your Seriously Ill Loved One is Unreasonable

My husband was truly heroic throughout his illness. In the face of the immense pain he endured, I know full well that I wouldn't have been able to be half as thoughtful and kind as he was. But as a person gets sicker and their pain increases, the drugs a doctor is likely to prescribe can seriously mess with a patient's mind. I knew this, so when my husband got tense or irritable, I let it pass. Generally, that is what I believe we caregivers are called to do.

However, there are times we *do* need to speak up. In my opinion, they occur when your spouse or loved one violates something that has been a cornerstone of your marriage or family life. You might call them the "unwritten rules" – and they are different for everyone.

Here's what I mean. My husband and I were very compatible, and we rarely argued. From the beginning of our marriage, when Stu was in the Navy and his ship was preparing for deployment by putting out to sea during the week and coming into port on weekends, we realized that trying to make each weekend like a "date" wasn't going to cut it. If we had to take care of something, we took care of it. If we needed to discuss something, we discussed it.

Through our entire marriage, my husband was always respectful, and the two of us were always able to talk things out in a reasonable way. We never ever, ever, talked to others about one another, we never argued in public, and we definitely did not yell at each other. I'm not saying we never got irritated with one another, but we didn't yell. However, suddenly, three out-of-character instances happened in relatively rapid succession.

The first time Stu yelled at me was in front of a nurse. I was shocked. This wasn't like him. He was in the hospital and had asked me to visit before I went to work, at lunch, and after work. At night, I had to run home and feed and walk the dogs before coming to the hospital. To say I was exhausted after more than a week of this is an understatement.

One night, I sank in the chair beside his bed and a nurse came in and began fishing around in his blanket for the cord to a wound care vacuum to which he was connected. Stu looked over at me and said in exasperation, "HELP HER!"

After she left, I should have told him that he had embarrassed me; that I was exhausted with all the running back and forth to the hospital after working all day myself. The nurse was doing what she was paid to do on her job, just like I did on mine. But I didn't. I attributed his out-of-character behavior to drugs and pain. He proudly told me that the nurses said he was an excellent patient because he never asked for anything. I knew that was because he waited for me to come and asked me to do what he needed! I understood he felt a loss of control and this was helpful to him … so I let it go.

The second time he yelled at me, we were outside that same hospital and having trouble with his wheelchair. A man turned around at the sound and caught my eye, and I thought, "Great. He thinks I'm an abused wife." But I understood that Stu was frustrated, and I knew he was in pain…so I let it go.

The final time, Stu was in yet another hospital recovering from a heart incident. He had asked me to go across the street to get him a sandwich at a deli. As I walked into the room, I realized I had forgotten to buy something for the home health aide we had hired during the last few months of my husband's illnesses. I apologized and gave her some money. He yelled at me because he didn't think it was enough.

I waited until the aide left, and this time I let him have it! He immediately apologized, but because I had bottled up my feelings for so long, his easy apology wasn't enough! I let him know exactly how I was feeling. Afterwards, I felt like a terrible person.

Lesson Learned: After writing about these past three incidents, I realized that they upset me because Stu had embarrassed me in public. We just didn't do that. I could and should have said something the first time he yelled. I knew Stu never had a hard time apologizing when he was wrong. In addition to his sense of humor and his spirit of adventure, it was one of the reasons I married him! If I had told him how tired I was and explained that he had embarrassed me, I know he would have apologized. But I didn't.

As a caregiver, you have to have compassion with a loved one who is seriously ill. You have to understand, especially when something is out of character, that it is often the drugs that are talking. Still, if something is important to you – i.e., it is not acceptable to yell at each other, especially in public – then, you need to bring it up. Nicely, but firmly. Otherwise, take it from me, your attempt at "saintly" behavior may very well backfire.

Lesson Learned: If your loved one really starts to behave unreasonably, don't bottle up your feelings until you explode. Wait for a moment when you are both calm – then have a reasonable discussion about it. The discussion doesn't have to last more than a few minutes, and neither of you should get upset. Just briefly remind them that this illness is affecting you, too, and that they hurt you when they said or did something. Clear the air! Chances are good that your loved one had no idea they upset you.

Chemo Brain

To cure Stu of leukemia, he underwent something like four or five rounds of chemotherapy. As anyone who has ever had a series of chemotherapy or radiation treatments knows, you don't just leap out of bed and start dancing. There are usually infections and other complications, and it takes time for the body, which has been poisoned, to regain its strength.

Stu finished his chemo in September 2008. We closed on our house in Pennsylvania in mid-September and a house in Alabama at the end of September. There was joy in getting into our beautiful "new to us" house, which is on a lake with lots of birds, ducks, geese, and fish. It made me happy to think that Stu would have a beautiful view to enjoy during his recovery.

However, chemotherapy kills a lot of a person's brain cells. "Chemo brain," as it is popularly called, is a real thing. Here's how I know: My husband was a physics teacher. To do that job, you have to take a test, which very few teachers do because it's so hard. My brilliant husband, who could calculate numbers in his head even faster than a calculator, didn't even study for the test he took in Pennsylvania. It was easy for him. He didn't understand why more people didn't take that test since physics teachers were in demand. He also passed the test in Alabama, but this time he had to study. It was harder for him.

Chemo has many other side effects. It can cause sleep disruptions, fatigue, and depression, which Stu fought. He wanted to return to teaching but, truthfully, he wasn't up to it. He started looking into beekeeping and other hobbies. There was just so much life in this man.

With the move, which was positive but stressful, the chemotherapy and its side effects, as well as Stu's close brush with death, I think we were both more exhausted than we realized. We both tried to get back to "normal." We took walks in the evening and talked a bit about the future, something you just don't do when your spouse is in danger of dying.

Finding Joy

To help us both rest and recuperate, we decided to go on a vacation, something we had missed the prior year. We picked an all-inclusive resort in Jamaica in February. It was awesome! We had a handicapped room, which was helpful; it had a beautiful balcony overlooking the resort and the ocean. There was also a huge infinity pool that extended from just outside the hotel lobby to what appeared to be the edge of the ocean, as well as a Lazy River.

But what I most remember was my husband's indomitable spirit. Stu was a strong swimmer and loved the ocean where he could feel weightless. Although he had difficulty walking on the sand and standing upright in the water because of his leg, he wasn't going to let such minor issues stop him.

We put the hotel lounge chairs as close to the water as possible. Stu managed to get into the water fairly quickly. Getting out was harder. He wasn't steady on that leg, and the sand and the pull of the ocean made it impossible for him to get out in the normal way. He ended up having to crawl up to the chair. The potential for humiliation like that would keep most people from attempting to get in the water.

But unlike many people, Stu didn't care what others thought. If he wanted to swim; he did. If he had to crawl on the sand to get back to his chair, that was the price he paid. I learned a lot from this amazing man whose spirit was always so alive.

Stu had eight months where he seemed to be cancer-free. Unfortunately, remission didn't last.

Lesson Learned: Understand that powerful drugs, like chemotherapy, have long-term effects. Don't expect your loved one to immediately snap back to their normal selves. Be patient. If possible, go for a change of scenery. Take some time to rest and recharge.

Lesson Learned: Before we discovered that Stu had cancer, back when we still thought of him as healthy and the "wound" on the bottom of his foot an aberration, he was placed in a walking cast and then a wheelchair. We were kind of embarrassed. We wanted everyone to know this was temporary. But as things got serious, embarrassment over the disabilities that cropped up during Stu's illnesses went away. Once we understood what was truly happening, Stu never let embarrassment over his disabilities get in the way of having a good time. That is my definition of "cool!"

REFLECTION QUESTIONS

- How have I reacted when my loved one is being unreasonable?

- How might I have handled things differently?

- What might I do if and when a similar situation presents itself in the future?

PRAYER:

Dear Jesus, there are so many ways for us to "be there" for a loved one when they fall. Help us to listen when they need to discuss options, while always respecting that the decision is ultimately theirs to make. Help us to look for ways to help our loved ones emotionally after their system has been battered or poisoned by powerful drugs and not to expect more from them than they are able to give. When they are unreasonable, help us to say something kindly but firmly, so our own emotions don't spiral out of control. And most of all, help us never to let embarrassment over a loved one's disabilities prevent us from enjoying the blessings that you make available in our lives. Amen.

Our Lady, Queen of Peace,
pray for us.

STATION OF THE CROSS:
Jesus Falls a Third Time

How many times did Jesus have to fall on the road to Calvary? Weren't two falls enough? God the Father knew that those of us still struggling on earth would need to see our Savior suffering as much or more than we do. Knowing that Jesus was willing to fall three times for us makes it easier for us to be willing to do the same for Him. Yes, He was God, but as this third fall shows, as true God and true man, Jesus also allowed Himself to be weighed down by the limitations of our human nature.

As anyone with a serious illness knows, the falls and disappointments are numerous. My loved one is now faced with a third bout of cancer. Two falls weren't enough for Jesus. God has asked one more from the two of us as well.

✝

Chapter 11

We Try for a Miracle

"Father, if thou art willing, remove this cup from me;
nevertheless not my will, but thine, be done."
- Luke 22:42 (RSVCE)

It was March 2009 when Stu noticed a bump just below his ankle bone. Wanting to take no chances, we went to see a medical oncologist at UAB. This doctor looked at Stu's leg, which was swollen from lymphedema and which leaked lymph fluid, and with a look of absolute revulsion on his face, said contemptuously, "You've got to get that thing off," meaning his leg.

I remember catching Stu's eye at the time, seeing the look of dismay on his face, and shaking my head so only Stu could see. Your loved one is a human being who deserves respect. We couldn't get out of there fast enough. Should I have said something to that "doctor?" I think we were both too shocked.

After that visit, Stu and I sat in our car, outside of my office. He wondered if he should get his leg "lopped off" like the doctor suggested. It took me a while to help my husband get his equilibrium back. We decided to get a second opinion.

In April, that "second opinion" doctor decided to operate. He hoped to remove the lump and clean up any cancer that might be there. Unfortunately, he couldn't get a clean margin – and we never would again. The cancer had spread, probably because the chemo which had killed the leukemia zeroed out Stu's immune system and allowed the melanoma to come roaring back.

What to do? What to do?

We Try For a Miracle

During the course of Stu's illness, we never stopped asking the Lord to physically cure Stu, if it be His Will. We knew, of course, that the reason something is considered a miracle is because it's not a common occurrence. But we also knew that there are many places in the Bible where Our Lord showed that He values persistence.

Think of the corrupt judge who didn't want to help the poor widow but ended up doing so because her persistence convinced him that, if he didn't help her, she might do him some harm or at least wear him out. As Our Lord says: *"Hear what the unrighteous judge says. And will not God vindicate His elect, who cry to Him day and night? Will He delay long over them? I tell you, He will vindicate them speedily."* Luke 18: 6-8 (RSV)

So, we visited the National Centre for Padre Pio in Barto, Pennsylvania, where we were allowed to pray holding St. Pio's bloody glove, which is a first- and second-class relic.

We also attended healing services, prayed with other relics of various saints, and said many novenas, including the Novena to St. Peregrine, patron of cancer patients, whose own cancerous leg was miraculously healed. We were also prayed over by many amazing people, including Sister Briege McKenna, whom I mentioned earlier.

When Stu's melanoma reappeared, I was blessed as EWTN's Communications Director to do a telephone interview with

Deacon John "Jack" Sullivan, the man whose miracle was responsible for Cardinal John Henry Newman's canonization. In the course of that interview, he asked me about myself, and we got on the subject of my husband's cancer.

Deacon Jack generously offered to pray over my husband with a relic of St. John Henry Newman, and I immediately accepted. We left for the Deacon's hometown of Plymouth, Massachusetts, almost as soon as we could get a flight!

Plymouth is an historic town on the Atlantic Ocean. We stayed in a wonderful downtown hotel, met Deacon Jack at a waterside restaurant for a lobster lunch, and he generously toured us around his town.

We then attended a healing service, and the Deacon prayed over my husband. We were so hopeful. We had a couple of beautiful days, but unfortunately, a physical healing was not part of God's plan for us.

When God's Plan is Not to Grant a Miracle

Right now, I think it's helpful to understand an important spiritual reality. You are facing the same fear that I did: your loved one may die. You asked for a miracle, and God didn't grant it. How should you think about that? After all, didn't Jesus say that God would hear the persistent widow?

He did indeed. The Bible also tells us that God the Father "heard" His Son when he cried out to him in torment, and that he "gave him victory over death" because He loved Him. Yet Jesus died a horrible death on the cross. So, what exactly does it mean when the Bible tells us that God "hears" us?

Remember the story of the paralyzed man whose friends lowered him through the roof of the place where Jesus was. Jesus surprises his friends – and us – when He says to the paralyzed man: "Your sins are forgiven." When the crowd gets riled up about that, He responds by saying: "Which is easier to say? Your sins are forgiven or arise and walk. But so that you may believe that the Son of God has power over sin and death, I say to you arise and walk."

Anytime you pray to the Lord, *something* happens. It may not be what you've asked for, but it will be what He knows you really need. God didn't heal Stu physically.

Yet He tells us in the parable above what's *really* important. In the light of Eternity, our lives here on earth are over in the blink of an eye. What *matters* is attaining heaven or spending as little time as possible in purgatory – or avoiding purgatory all together. And there's only one way to do that and that's to unite your will with God's will, no matter how hard it is.

Before His Passion, Jesus said to the Father in the Garden of Gethsemane: *"Father, if Thou art willing, remove this cup from Me; nevertheless not My will, but Thine, be done."* Luke 22:42 (RSV)

Are you and I, the servants, greater than the Master? Should we demand that the Father do more for us than He did for His own Son?

God has His reasons for illness and death. In the case of Jesus, He wanted to save all of us from eternal death, which is hell.

For what or for whom might Jesus *need* to use *your* suffering? It's an awesome question to ponder! It gives your suffering cosmic meaning!

But does suffering do anything for us as individuals?

You better believe it! Do you sometimes, maybe many times, wish you were more patient, kinder, and more courageous? Do you wish you had the fortitude to persevere when the going gets tough, or the ability to counsel those who are in trouble? Do you want to be someone who keeps the faith even when, especially when, things get really difficult?

The Lord allows illness in our own life or that of our loved one because He wants to give you these and many other gifts. That's why I say you can't do this alone. You must realize by now that, like Jesus, we are not just fighting a physical battle. We're fighting a spiritual battle, so we need to put on our spiritual armor *every day* in order to fight bravely!

St. Paul tells us that athletes run so as to win a race and crown of leaves that withers. We should run to win the race, which is Eternal Life!

So how do we prepare ourselves to win this battle? How do we put on the Armor of God? We'll talk about that in the next chapter.

REFLECTION QUESTIONS

- Think: What blessings have I received over the course of this illness from other people or from circumstances that have worked out better than I could have hoped?

- What gifts might the Lord be giving me or my loved one as a result of this illness? Am I more patient, loving, stronger, wiser, a better spouse/parent/sibling/friend?

PRAYER:

Father, just as You did on your way to Calvary, we face a third "fall." You know very well how badly we want You to take away this illness. Nevertheless, we ask you to help us pray as Your Son did in the Garden of Gethsemane: If it be possible, let this cup pass from us, but—and we ask for the grace to mean this – not our will, but Thine be done. Please help my loved one and me to see beyond this "fall." Make us aware of the blessings You are sending us, and help us to remember to offer up this suffering, just as You did, for the salvation of the world. In Jesus' Name we pray. Amen.

Our Lady of Hope,
pray for us.

Chapter 12

How to Put on the Armor of God

"Be strong in the Lord and in the strength of his might.
Put on the whole armor of God,
that you may be able to stand against the wiles of the devil."
- Ephesians 6: 10-11 (RSV)

In the last chapter, we talked about standing strong in the Lord by putting on the Armor of God. There are many ways to do this.

Here are a few:

Pray (Of Course!):

My sister Marian used to get up each morning and literally "mime" putting on the helmet of salvation, the breastplate of righteousness, the belt of truth, the shoes of peace, the shield of faith, and the sword of the Holy Spirit. Then, she would begin her day!

Where did she get this? Take a moment to read Ephesians 6:10-17 (RSVCE). Among other things, it says:

"Finally, be strong in the Lord and in the strength of his might. Put on the whole armor of God, that you may be able to stand against the wiles of the devil. For we are not contending against flesh and blood, but against the principalities, against the powers, against the world rulers of this present darkness, against the spiritual hosts of wickedness in the heavenly places. Therefore take the whole armor of God, that you may be able to withstand in the evil day, and having done all, to stand. Stand therefore, having girded your loins with truth, and having put on the breastplate of righteousness, and having shod your feet with the equipment of the gospel of peace; above all taking the shield of faith, with which you can quench all the flaming darts of the evil one. And take the helmet of salvation, and the sword of the Spirit, which is the word of God."

Befriend Your Guardian Angel – and Your Patron Saint

You probably learned the Guardian Angel prayer as a child, but may have abandoned it. It goes like this:

> *"Angel of God, my Guardian dear,*
> *to whom God's love commits me here.*
> *Ever this day be at my side, to light and guard,*
> *to rule and guide.*
> *Amen."*

Don't forget, your Angel's job is to help you. Ask for his/her assistance.

The prayer to St. Michael the Archangel is especially powerful.

> *St. Michael the Archangel, defend us in battle.*
> *Be our protection against the*
> *wickedness and snares of the devil.*
> *May God rebuke him, we humbly pray.*
> *And do thou, O Prince of the Heavenly Host,*
> *by the power of God,*
> *cast into hell Satan, and all the evil spirits,*
> *who prowl about the world*
> *seeking the ruin of souls.*
>
> *Amen.*

My full name is Michelleanne Christine Maria Laque Johnson – so my patron saints are St. Michael, St. Anne, Jesus Christ, and Our Lady! Don't forget to pray to yours as well. There is a reason we have our names – and it's not just because it was your grandmother's name, or that your mother liked a particular actor! Something else was at work, if only with your Confirmation Name, which is very important!

Don't Forget Your Morning Offering

As a secular Carmelite, I particularly love the following Morning Offering – and notice, as you and I continue our walk to Calvary, that this prayer mentions the Precious Blood of Jesus in the first sentence:

Oh my God, in union with the Immaculate Heart of Mary
(kiss your Scapular, which we'll discuss in a minute),
I offer You the Precious Blood of Jesus from all the altars
throughout the world, joining with it the offering of
my every thought, word, and action of this day.

"Oh, My Jesus, I desire to gain every indulgence
(I add merit, grace, and blessing) it is possible to gain,
and I offer it (them), together with myself, to
Mary Immaculate, that she may best apply it (them)
to the interests of Your Most Sacred Heart.

Precious Blood of Jesus, save us.
Immaculate Heart of Mary, pray for us.
Sacred Heart of Jesus, have mercy on us.

Amen

Novenas

Believe it or not, there is a 10-word emergency novena that you can say on the fly, nine times. This was given to me by a wonderful nun. Here it is: "Jesus, I surrender myself to you. Take care of everything." You could alter it to say: Take care of x situation, or my loved one, or this doctor who might be a problem. By the way, I like to add one more word: "Please" take care of everything!

Spiritual Warfare Prayers

There is a very small booklet called, *Spiritual Warfare Prayers*, put out by Valentine Publishing House, which is a tiny treasure trove of prayers to say when the enemy is doing his best to disturb your peace. Purchase it online.

Journaling

Having a hard time concentrating? I admit I had never really seriously tried journaling. But during Stu's illness, it quickly became important to me. Because my mind felt so scattered, I felt like I wasn't praying well, so I started to write down what I wanted to say – almost so I could prove to myself that I was praying.

Fortunately, I had been told at some point in my life that a good way to journal is to first, write down your own thoughts and second, to write down what you think Jesus would say to you in response.

If you've never done this, I highly recommend it. It was amazing how much wisdom would flow across the page as I imagined what Jesus would say. I know there were many times the words I wrote weren't coming from me. They were inspired by the Holy Spirit.

As I read over some of my journal entries over those years, I realize in retrospect that some of the prayers I was saying at the time were the best of my life! Here's an example:

> *Dear God, I love my husband more than myself. I don't want him to suffer. I want him to be happy. I want heaven for him. I want him to be close to You. I want him to attain a high degree of glory. Please show me what I can do for him spiritually in these last days. Even though I've*

had a hard time praying myself, I ask You to help him to pray well.

I want to pray well, too. I want to hear You because I know You have the words of eternal life. Show us "the way." Help us to walk this path to Calvary with You, Jesus. Mary, my Mother, help me to be strong and courageous like you, standing beside my husband, helping him to accept God's will. Jesus, please give me strength and courage. Help me not to waste time on what is not important.

I don't see or understand the Divine Plan for our lives. But it is enough to know that You do. You hold our lives in Your hands. Some day we will understand why things had to be. We will see life from Your perspective.

For now, please pour out your Grace upon us and help us to correspond to that Grace. Help me to face this with courage, Lord, with faith, with every gift of the Holy Spirit, and, most of all, help my husband to do the same. Show me how to help him.

Amen.

I always felt better after journaling, even though, objectively, my circumstances hadn't changed. I encourage you to try it.

Sacraments

The highest form of prayer is the Mass, which includes the sacrament of Holy Communion. The ability to receive Christ in person will strengthen you in a way that nothing else can. Remind yourself that when you receive Jesus, He is now physically part of you; He's in your heart, your mind, and your spirit, loving you and helping you carry your cross. Trust that. Jesus will reward that trust.

Sacramentals

Friends, don't forget to protect yourself by wearing blessed objects such as a Miraculous Medal and/or a Brown Scapular, which are my personal favorites. Sometimes, we Catholics wear these sacramentals and forget the incredible promises associated with them. Take a look!

> **Brown Scapular Promise:** "Whosoever dies wearing it shall not suffer eternal fire. It shall be a sign of salvation, a protection in danger and pledge of peace." So make sure both you and your loved one are wearing it, especially when they are near death!

> **Miraculous Medal Promises:** In explaining what the medal should look like to St. Catherine Labouré, Our Lady said: "These rays symbolize the graces I shed upon those who ask for them. The gems from which rays do not fall are the graces for which souls forget to ask." So, let's not forget! She also said: "All who wear it [the medal] will receive great graces; they should wear it around the neck. Graces will abound for persons who wear it with confidence."

Spiritual Reading

When we are in crisis, big spiritual tomes are not what most of us need. We need to read things that are reassuring and faith-affirming. It's important for you, as the caregiver, and it's important for your loved one, since your #1 job is to help get him or her to heaven!

As a secular Carmelite, I turn to the saints of my own order. Brother Lawrence of the Resurrection, for example, wrote a short, easy-to-read treasure called, *The Practice of the Presence of God,* which tells you very simply how to keep God's Presence with you through the ordinary course of your day. I also love *Divine Mercy in My Soul,* the Diary of St. Faustina, a Mercy sister.

While the saints had a lot to say about suffering, I find myself remembering a story about a saint who had a vision in which her enemies were arrayed about her. That's when she realized that their slings and arrows actually were helping her to ascend the staircase to heaven much more quickly! As caregivers, we think of the enemy as our loved one's illness, but be assured when you lean on God and do all you humanly can to fight this battle with your loved one, this "enemy" will also help you get to heaven much faster if you let it!

And speaking of heaven, I'd like to recommend Anthony DeStefano's book, *A Travel Guide to Heaven*, a biblically correct but fun read on exactly what heaven is going to be like – and it's probably like nothing like you have ever imagined! In the final year of his life, I read a chapter a night to Stu and we discussed it. It was a beautiful time for us.

Bible quotes and quotes from saints can also be very helpful during this time. On page 100 of the book, *St. Therese of Lisieux: Her Last Conversations*, the saint gives this reply to Mother Agnes of Jesus after she expresses her concern that that the young girl is going to suffer a lot before she dies: "Why fear in advance? Wait at least for it to happen before having any distress. Don't you see that I would begin to torment myself by thinking that, if persecutions and massacres come, as they are predicted, someone will perhaps snatch out your eyes."

St. Therese is talking about anticipatory suffering, something of which we are all guilty. In more modern terms, the saint is telling us: Don't borrow trouble! Trouble may not come at all, and, even if it does, worrying about it not only doesn't help, but it may bring it about sooner than later.

You can find many more examples of books and quotes like these, just by doing simple searches for things like "suffering (or courage) psalms proverbs," or "suffering catholic saints." Even better, go to the EWTN Religious Catalogue site (https://www. ewtnreligiouscatalogue.com) and type in "suffering." Tons of religious reading and videos will pop up.

Unlike secular reading, spiritual reading should be done very slowly. Read St. Therese's quote and sit with it for a few minutes. Ponder it as our Blessed Mother pondered through so much of her life. What is the Lord telling you through this saint? Spend 5, 10, or 15 minutes each day with such material; it's not a huge amount of time, and you will be richly blessed.

REFLECTION QUESTION

- Of the many things listed in this chapter, which one or ones do I think I would be most helpful to me, and how might I begin to incorporate them into my daily life?

PRAYER:

Father, please help us to put on the Armor of God as You commanded so that we may fight bravely, rising after each fall to continue the battle You have given us to fight. And, having fought bravely, may we one day join You and all our loved ones in the Kingdom of Heaven where there is no sorrow and no pain, but only Eternal Joy. We ask this in Jesus' name. Amen.

Our Lady of Mount Carmel, Vanquisher of Satan, pray for us.

In Sickness and in Health

My high school years were spent on a Naval Base in Rota, Spain, so I saw lots of weddings with the Arch of Swords. So cool! My secret dream to have such a ceremony was fulfilled the day I married Stu.

Stu and I posed for a photo after placing my wedding bouquet before the Blessed Mother and consecrating our marriage to her.

The man in the white uniform furthest to the right is the late Navy Chaplain Fr. Brian Kane. He would marry my two sisters and me – all within six months! The other men in uniform were Stu's buddies from the Naval Academy. Stu was a humble man, but to me he was a real cutie – and he would always remain cute to me, even when he got sick and gained weight.

At Home

At Left: Stu outside our first apartment in San Diego. Most California apartment complexes have pools, and ours was right behind all those palm trees.

Stu at a lake near our apartment in La Mesa, California, where we lived during the early years of our marriage.

Left: I love dogs, but Stu was obsessed. Here are two of our favorites over the 35 years we were married! Winston (white), a Samoyed who was embarrassed by his haircut, and Bosley, a rescue who was devoted to Stu and his tennis ball.

On Vacation

At Right: I remember the first time Stu asked where we were going on vacation. My family didn't take regular vacations but Stu's did, so I learned from him how important they are! This photo is taken outside our little bungalow at a resort in Jamaica.

At Right: As an editor for a secular publication, my job took me to a conference in Vail, Colorado. Stu came with me, and we went snowmobiling for the first and last time in our lives! The suits kept us from freezing. In this photo, we had stopped for hot chocolate.

I think this photo was taken in Maine. We went shortly after a surgeon removed many cancerous lymph nodes from Stu's groin. His cancerous leg had to be wrapped so I knew our usual beach vacation would be too hot for him. Maine's scenery and relatively cool climate (even in August) were a Godsend!

Under a waterfall in Jamaica-we climbed up the waterfall with a group. Stu was a very strong man, and I was always proud of him for helping those who struggled – including me!

At Left: Stu as a young man with his grandparents, Maddie and Marshall Green. His grandmother told me when Stu was young, he thought his grandfather was in law enforcement because his name was Marshall!

Stu graduating from the Naval Academy in Annapolis, Maryland.

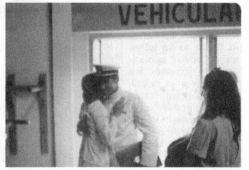

Stu and his Mom Carolyn hugging after the graduation ceremony. (I am in in the blue jacket to the right.)

Stu playing with Winston as a puppy: It still cracks me up to see how small the dog was, especially compared to my very strong and fit young husband.

✝

Chapter 13

Making the Best of Hard Times

"And [Jesus] said to all, 'If any man would come after me, let
him deny himself and take up his cross daily and follow me.'"
- Luke 9:23(RSVCE)

While the Lord did not miraculously cure my husband, He did show us the next important step on our journey. After much prayer, we made the decision to go to what is widely considered to be the Holy Grail of cancer hospitals: MD Anderson in Houston, Texas.

Here's where having records from all the hospitals we had visited, including copies of Stu's X-rays, CT Scans, and MRIs, would have saved me untold hours at a point when time was not on our side. As I mentioned previously, I would eventually set up a "medicine closet" with all of these things and more, but at that point I had to make a lot of phone calls and visit a lot of hospital records rooms to get these records.

Once Stu's records were sent to MD Anderson, my husband was accepted as a patient. For six months, we made the 10-hour trip by car (not counting stops), usually stopping halfway for the night. We couldn't fly because flying can exacerbate lymphedema; in other words, make his swollen leg even worse.

For most of our marriage, Stu had insisted on doing the driving, which was fine with me. But over the next six months, I was the one who began driving most of the way. I am an impatient driver – not proud of it. But here's where I had to learn patience. I often had to drive slowly, in an attempt to avoid bumps because it was painful for Stu.

We had one incident which, in retrospect, would be funny if it hadn't been so serious. Stu had just had another operation after he, once again, had a patch of skin surgically grafted onto the heel of his foot. Afterwards, he was given something called vacuum-assisted closure therapy. In layman's terms, that meant a machine was attached to his heel, which kept the wound dry and helped insure that the graft would firmly attach itself to his heel. We were told if we lost that vacuum seal, we had something like two minutes to restore it or the graft would fail!

Imagine this. Stu sat in the back seat with his foot set on a pillow. The highway was fairly smooth, but sometimes, over the hundreds of miles we traveled, the car would jounce a little. So at least three times, the alarm on the machine started shrieking, which meant the vacuum seal had broken.

I immediately had to pull over to the side of the road with my heart in my throat, leap out of the front seat, yank open the back door, and, as quickly as humanly possible, reposition the vacuum over the graft to restore the suction. If Stu were alive, I can imagine us laughing about this now! But, at the time, it was anything but funny.

Can you see, though, how experiences like this would bond us? When you're working together like this with your spouse, you can't help but get closer. So, despite everything, it was ultimately a blessing!

Lesson Learned: Working together to defeat a common enemy – your loved one's illness – can help forge an even stronger bond with your loved one. That's just one more potential blessing in these hard times!

MD Anderson

So, what is MD Anderson really like? First of all, it's huge, a cluster of high-rise buildings and wide hallways. I think of it, even now, as a city – a city of cancer patients – all fighting for their lives. All of the doctors we met there were extremely competent. Treatment was state-of-the-art. There are probably hundreds of clinical trials going on there at any one time.

Patients we met were invariably kind and helpful to each other. Many of the hotels in the area cater to MD Anderson patients, so we met fellow patients in our hotel, on the hotel shuttle to the hospital, and in the hospital itself. Everyone shared what they knew.

It was on our hotel shuttle that we met the man I mentioned earlier in this book, whose head was blown up like a balloon. His wife told us that he had refused to go to a doctor when he first realized something was wrong. Undoubtedly, he was afraid. But now, he was in danger of losing both his eyesight and his hearing.

> **Lesson Learned:** If you know something is physically wrong with you, especially if you're afraid it's cancer, don't let fear keep you from going to the doctor and finding out. Pretending it's not there doesn't make it go away. The earlier you seek treatment, the better the potential outcome.

We also met a young woman from Hawaii who was going through cancer treatments all by herself. Her husband was back home, working. She was terrified before the first chemotherapy session. We couldn't go with her because Stu had his own appointments, but my husband and I were able to provide her with some much-needed moral support during the time we were together.

> **Lesson Learned:** By helping others, we often help ourselves. As you're going through these hard times, you will meet others whose cross may be even heavier than your own – or someone who is having a harder time carrying their cross than you are. Reach out! Be a Simon of Cyrene for those you meet. You will be glad you did.

MD Anderson Surgeries

Stu had a number of operations while at MD Anderson. One surgeon performed a complicated operation in Stu's abdominal area. That surgeon later told us he didn't believe anyone else in the world could have successfully performed that operation. That's not modest, but I have to tell you, I have no doubt it was true.

Stu did seem to get some of his energy back, although his leg was still filled with cancer, as were other parts of his body. We knew this was a temporary respite, but it gave us hope that he would remain alive awhile longer – and the longer he was alive, the better the chance that someone would discover a cure. That was always our hope.

As Christmas 2009 neared, the hospital did what they could to make things a bit more festive. The hospital lobby was filled with carolers singing and crafters selling items that people could purchase for Christmas gifts. I remember being aware of that as I walked through the lobby and thinking it was nice that they had tried to do something for patients and their families. But I was also aware of the contrast between the battle patients were fighting and the more secular joys of the Christmas season.

The Perfect Gift For the Homebound

Here, I am reminded of an extremely kind thing my sister Marian and her husband Mike did for Stu and me for Christmas 2009. We usually went to the Virginia/Maryland area during Christmas because that's where most of our family members were located at the time. But that year, Stu wasn't up to it.

My sister made us promise not to touch her gifts for us until Christmas day. When we finally opened them, we found two iPods, which, at the time, were the latest in technology. We spent a good portion of the day setting them up with songs that we both enjoyed.

Lesson Learned: If you are looking for a gift for a loved one, or if you know a couple going through a serious illness, a gift that takes their minds off of the illness is of inestimable value! Music tends to do that!

Caring for Yourself

We learned a lot of valuable lessons on those 10-hour drives to MD Anderson. When you must travel, here are some suggestions to help you find a bit of joy:

- Get a good book. I've talked about spiritual reading, but sometimes you just need to find a book that is set in a fun place you want to visit – an island, a beach town, a mountaintop resort – and get LOST. It needs to be a book that is sure to have a happy ending. If you're driving, get an audio book. The benefit is that both the driver and the passenger can potentially enjoy the book. Today, you can even check out audio books through your local library. The car isn't the only place to enjoy a good book. As a caregiver you will quickly learn that a lot of your time will be spent waiting: waiting for your loved one to see a doctor; waiting for surgery to be completed; waiting to get a prescription. A good book is a huge stress reliever.

- If reading or listening to books isn't your thing, choose another hobby. Listen to a podcast or watch a movie – something fun, but nothing heavy. You're dealing with enough stress.

- Exercise, get outside. If you're going to stay in a hotel, find one with a gym or one that is located in a place where you can safely take a walk outside in the fresh air. What a pleasure it is to be outside those hospital walls! As a caregiver, you will often have to exercise alone while your loved one rests. That's a good use of your time.

- When Stu could no longer walk farther than out to the car, and he was up to it, he would join me on his electric scooter. The two of us together, outside, talking. Nice.

- If you're driving, do a quick internet search or use a AAA guidebook to find a fun restaurant along the route; anything to add a little joy to what can be a pretty grim experience. I remember one really special lunch we had at an historic home in Mississippi when Stu was still well enough to enjoy it.

I want to keep reminding you: your loved one is still here!

- If you're going to be in another town for a few days, and your loved one is up to it, try to make time to do one fun thing. Take a drive, go to a local park. During one stint at MD Anderson, I remember visiting a replica of a nearby "frontier town," where we had lunch. We ate ice cream on an outside bench, and I took a moment to wander into a nearby store and buy a pretty bracelet. Make memories!

- Bring some good music in the car and rock out. Sing together. I remember Stu liked to put on classical music and pretend he was conducting an orchestra. I still smile when I think of him acting so silly!

- Spend time talking to family and friends, but only when it's helpful. If you don't want to keep repeating the same thing, sign up for a site like Caring Bridge, https://www. caringbridge.org/, where you or a loved one can post updates for those you allow to access your page.

Lesson Learned: We didn't know it at the time, but Stu still had two-and-a-half more years to live. What if we had not made the most of this time? What a terrible waste that would have been – so many blessings would have been lost!

Find a Good Hotel

Part of caring for yourself is finding a decent place to stay. Here are some tips when you have to go out of state to get care, which means you're going to have to stay at least overnight, maybe a couple nights, in a hotel.

- Money obviously dictates what you can do, but, if possible, try not to cheap out too much. Today, there are plenty of rewards cards (either travel rewards cards or hotel rewards cards or both) that you can use to make your stay more economical.

- Many big hospitals have hotels that are connected to them. There's a lot to be said for that in terms of convenience. At MD Anderson, patients can get blood work and other basic procedures done in the lobby of the connected hotel, saving lots of time and stress. We didn't realize that until later in our journey.

- The hotel we usually stayed at in Houston wasn't fancy, but it was clean and reasonably priced. It featured a free shuttle, which saved us money on gas and parking fees, and a small kitchen, which saved on food. We even signed up for the local grocery store so we could get discounts. Because the hotel specialized in helping MD Anderson patients (many of whom stayed for months), they also offered free movies and books, a tiny gym and indoor pool, and were steps away from a nearby restaurant. You have enough stress. Make it as easy on yourself as possible. Of course, the ability to do a lot of the above depends on your loved one's health. As we neared the end of our time in Houston, we stopped going to restaurants because Stu couldn't eat much. Instead, we opted to use the kitchenette in our hotel room, we ordered a pizza, or I went to a restaurant for takeout. One weekend, we drove to the Houston Zoo, but once we got there, Stu couldn't even get out of the car. I realized he had gone for my sake, but he really wasn't up to it. It's a balancing act.

When You Miss Doing the Things You Used to Do

At another point in our journey, my husband spent time at Lakeshore Rehabilitation Hospital in Alabama, which is located across the street from a beautiful mall with lots of wonderful restaurants. To give us a break from hospital food, I remember entering a deli that Stu and I enjoyed before he got sick to order some of their delicious sandwiches. As I stood there waiting for our order, I looked over at the tables where people were enjoying their meals and wished, for a moment, that I could just sit there for a few minutes, eating and reading a book. But even as that thought entered my mind, another followed. There will be plenty of time for that on the "other side."

And it's so true. Well-meaning friends will sometimes tell you to take more time for yourself. Of course, you must do the things you need to do to stay healthy. Exercise. Eat well. Get sleep when you can. Take time to talk to friends. You may also have others in the family who also need your attention. All of that is extremely important. You can't take care of others if you haven't taken care of yourself.

However, I'm telling you now; you will never regret the time you spend with your loved one. Giving up some of those small pleasures, making adjustments so you can include your loved one in whatever activity you miss doing, is more than worth it.

After Stu died, I had a conversation with a friend of mine whose husband was ill. She said she just wished she could go to a concert or a restaurant with friends. I remembered that moment in the deli and said to her: "I understand. But if he dies, you won't want to."

"Oh…" she breathed.

My fellow caregivers, I know this is hard, but please know that your love will never be more pure or more selfless than it is at this moment. This trial will teach you an immense amount; it will break you open and rebuild you into a more loving and more compassionate person – if you allow it!

I look back on those days, and I realize that love is most fully alive when it is being perfected. As hard as this is, it really is a foretaste of the love we will find in heaven. Just as Jesus loved us in the pain of His cross, so we must love others in our own pain.

I promise: You will be glad you put your loved one first when you're on the other side of this battle.

Lesson Learned: It's important to strike a balance between caring for yourself and caring for others. As the airlines say, "Put on your safety mask before helping others." You can't help others if you don't take care of yourself. At the same time, realize that this time will never come again. You will never regret giving up small pleasures for the sake of your beloved.

REFLECTION QUESTIONS

- Before my loved one got sick, what did the two of us enjoy doing together, and how can I either recreate that experience or create a similar experience? For example, if my loved one loved the outdoors but can no longer hike, what can I do to provide a fun, outdoor experience?

- What fun things can I find to make a long car trip more enjoyable?

- How am I caring for myself? What hobbies did I used to enjoy – reading, computer games, podcasts, audio books, knitting, socializing – that I could incorporate into all the waiting time that occurs when visiting doctors and hospitals?

- What gift could I give my loved one that he or she would enjoy while waiting to be seen by yet another doctor?

- If I've forgotten to include God in developing new experiences and thanking Him not only for the ideas He gives me, but for being with me and my loved one as we play, how can I remind myself to be more faithful in the future?

- What might I do to help someone in a similar situation, even if it's with some advice or a listening ear?

PRAYER:

Jesus, in reading about Your Passion or saying the Stations of the Cross, we see that You fell three times on the road to Calvary. However, You always got up because You knew that Your journey had not yet come to an end, and You yearned to offer Yourself up for our salvation. Like You, we still have further to go. Like You, we want to offer up our cross for the salvation of our families as well as for the world. However, in the midst of our own Passion, help us to see that blessings and good times are not only STILL available to us but that, in some cases, are ONLY available to us because of the cross You have asked us to bear. No matter what happens, please help us to see Your Love in every person we meet, and in every circumstance in which we find ourselves, and, in seeing Your Love, may we draw ever closer to You. In Jesus' precious name we pray. Amen.

Our Lady of Consolation, pray for us.

Chapter 14

Important Things to Do
Before Your Loved One Dies

*"I am the light of the world. He who follows me will not walk in
darkness, but will have the light of life."*
- John 8:12 (RSVCE)

This may seem like a strange time to interrupt our story to discuss
what to do before your loved one dies. But it's very important
to think about the following items before things get crazy – and
they *will* get crazy as your loved one gets closer to the end of
their life. For years, my husband and I could not bring ourselves
to talk about the possibility that he would die or, if he did, what
the funeral should look like. Although we never gave up hope, we
finally faced the fact that I needed to know what to do if and when
the Lord took him home.

Below are some of the more critical things you need to think about.

Prepare Sacramentally

Before your loved one dies, he or she should, if possible, receive:

- **The Anointing of the Sick, formerly known as Extreme
  Unction or the Last Rites**: The name was changed because
  many patients feared that receiving this sacrament meant

they would die. Actually, in some cases, the graces of this sacrament have caused patients to rebound. At worst, it prepares them for heaven; in other words, there is no downside.

- **The Sacrament of Reconciliation, also known as confession:** If you have time, get a good guide to confession and a priest you love and put him alone in the sick room with your loved one.

- **The Apostolic Blessing:** I had never heard of this, but my husband was blessed to receive this from EWTN's Fr. Joseph. Not only does the Blessing forgive sin, but the temporal punishment due to sin. This is huge! Author Susan Tassone, the Purgatory Lady, calls this the Deluxe Package to heaven. Any priest can impart this blessing but, for some reason, few do unless asked. Ask! It's the most incredible gift you can give you loved one before they die.

You and Your Loved One Should Also Recite:

- **The Divine Mercy Chaplet:** Jesus promises that anyone who recites this powerful prayer even once will meet Him as the Merciful Savior and not the Just Judge. Incredible! Jesus obviously wants us to join Him in heaven, which means He wants us to become saints. As EWTN's Mother Angelica would say: "Don't miss the opportunity."

- **The Rosary:** Are you aware of the 15 promises Our Lady makes to those who faithfully recite the Rosary? Among other things, Our Lady says souls that say the Rosary have a powerful armor against hell; shall not perish by an unprovided death; shall not die without the sacraments of the Church; shall participate in the merits of the saints in paradise at the moment of death; shall be delivered from Purgatory by Our Lady; shall merit a high degree of glory in heaven; and much more!

After Your Loved One Dies:

- **Have 30 Gregorian Masses said for your loved one's soul.** I learned about this from a conference on Purgatory with Susan Tassone (Author of *Day By Day for the Holy Souls in Purgatory, and much more)* at the Shrine of the Blessed Sacrament in Hanceville, Alabama. She said that Pope Gregory had a monk appear to him after his death to ask for prayers. The Pope had 30 Masses said for that monk, who afterwards appeared to him in glory. Thus began the tradition of having 30 Gregorian Masses said for the dead. I didn't find out about this until several years after Stu died. I have now had this done for my husband, my father, my sister, and others. Three popular sites that offer these Masses are the Pious Union of St. Joseph, the Seraphic Mass Association, and the National Shrine of Our Lady of Czestochowa (See "Resources" for more information).

Prepare Spiritually

See Chapter 12, Putting on the Armor of God. It's especially important right now that your loved one wear their Scapular because the promise is that: "Whoever dies wearing it shall not suffer eternal fire." The Miraculous Medal and Holy Water are also great sacramentals to have on hand at this time.

Prepare Your Loved One Emotionally

My husband was very worried about leaving me alone, and about all the things I would have to do after he died. I remember Stu, as the quadriplegic he would become, saying to me, "I hate to leave you alone in this terrible world." With one hand I grabbed his hand, placed the other on his cheek, and looking him in the eyes, I said: "Honey, you can't think you can take better care of me than Jesus. He will be with me. He is with me. It's okay." Your loved one needs to hear this.

Prepare Financially: Make Up a Book of Financial Records

If it's your spouse who is dying, you will undoubtedly be taking over more and more duties as he or she gets sicker. Realize, however, that there are going to be things that only your spouse knows. In many cases, these things are financial, so please allow me make a suggestion.

Pick up a 3-ring binder, some paper, plastic sheet protectors, and some index dividers with pockets and go through every financial record you have.

What bank accounts, retirement accounts, investment accounts, insurance accounts, or property do you own? Do you know the passwords and account numbers for all of these accounts? Are these accounts in both of your names? Are you, or some other family member, listed as the beneficiary on all your accounts? If not, the state will get a lot of the money. Is that what you want? What phone numbers should you call when your spouse dies?

In our case, every single account was placed in a separate section of the binder. On the paper, I wrote down the name of the account, account number, password(s), phone number(s), website, and account rep if we had one. Into the plastic sleeve went the contract, or the latest statement. Into the index divider pockets went any other miscellaneous items pertaining to the account.

This book was a lifesaver!

Unfortunately, even though we thought we were completely prepared, we still forgot a piece of land that Stu's father had bequeathed him out in Colorado. Unfortunately, it was in both my husband's name and his father's name. Both had died. Did I have to probate two estates for this? I didn't know. How expensive would it be? Try hard to think of *everything*; don't let this happen to you!

Prepare a Will

When Stu was actively dying, a very kind lawyer told us that if we had no children and everything was in both our names, I would be okay; that I could come see her after Stu's death. Unfortunately, we forgot the piece of property above. It was a thorn in my side for years!

If you don't have a will, for heaven's sake, get one. You can use a lawyer, a will preparation software, or a service such as LegalZoom. Just do it! You'll be glad you did.

Prepare for the Funeral

It took us a long time to get to this point, but Stu was sick for eight years. We eventually came to the point where we were able to discuss his death. Here are some things to consider:

- Does your loved one want to be cremated? There was a time this was not allowed in the Catholic Church, but it is now an option. However, the Church still prefers burial, and urges that the body be present for the funeral. If cremated, the ashes should remain together in a worthy container and be laid to rest with the Church's rites.

- Where should your loved one be buried? We had moved to Alabama, but my family was in Virginia and Maryland. Would I remain in Alabama after Stu died, or would I go "home"? I didn't know. We finally decided to bury Stu in Virginia, near my father's plot. I have two plots, one for Stu and one for me. I followed my mother's example in doing this when my father died.

- What are your spouse's favorite Scripture readings?

- What are your spouse's favorite hymns? My husband had been in the Navy, so he wanted the Navy Hymn sung!

- Who should sing these hymns?

- What priest do you want to be the main celebrant? What other priests should be there?

- Who should do the readings at the funeral Mass?

- Who should bring up the gifts?

- Who should the pallbearers be?

- Are you going to put an obituary in the paper? Which paper? Most newspapers now offer an online "book" which people from all over the country can sign, but it costs money. Do you want to do that?

- Who do you need to tell about the funeral? How will you get the word out? Usually, it's helpful to let people in different categories take over this chore. For example, your nuclear family tells your relatives, your HR department or your boss may alert people at work (sometimes you must alert multiple workplaces), your next-door neighbor may tell others in the community, you might alert your alumni magazine if that's an important group; a club that's important to you (Sr. Citizen's Center, Country Club, Sailing Club, Golf Club – the list of possibilities is endless).

- If you have children, are they old enough to attend? If not, who will care for them?

- If you have pets and you must travel, who will care for them?

If you have special circumstances, you may have to be creative. What do I mean by that?

In my case, my mother had an operation before Stu died, which left her unable to travel to Alabama, and my sister Yvonne is immune compromised, which makes travel very difficult for her. In addition, Stu went to the Naval Academy and taught high school in Pennsylvania, so a lot of our friends and family were up north. That's why I decided to have two funerals.

The first was in Alabama. That was attended by all my Alabama friends and co-workers from EWTN. My sister Marian and my brother Larry were also in attendance. Our priest friend, Fr. Paul, officiated at both Masses, but the Alabama Mass had the added benefit of being concelebrated by most of EWTN's friars. Such a blessing!

The second funeral was in Alexandria, Virginia. That was attended by my entire nuclear family; Stu's Naval Academy friends; the principal, teachers, and students from the high school at which he had taught; his sister and her family; and my own friends from Pennsylvania, which is where we had lived before moving to Alabama. Do whatever works best for you.

Obituary/Eulogy

While the Church's funeral rite doesn't permit a eulogy to replace the homily, a family member can be given a few moments to speak at the end of Mass, usually after Communion and before the final rites. (For more information, go online to https://www.usccb.org/prayer-and-worship/sacraments-and-sacramentals/bereavement-and-funerals/cremation-and-funerals.)

One thing I so wish I had done before Stu died is write his obituary and a eulogy. I was in no shape to write his obituary after his death. At the very least, consider making a list of the important things you want to cover in an obituary or eulogy if the time comes.

REFLECTION QUESTIONS

- What might I do today to help my loved one spiritually prepare to meet Our Lord?

- If my loved one is expressing anxiety over leaving me behind, have I thought about how I can give him or her "permission" to go "home"?

- Am I aware of all our financial accounts, and do I have the passwords, account numbers, and contact info for these accounts in one place?

- Do I know about life insurance or other money that might help with funeral expenses should that become necessary?

- Does my loved one have a will?

- Have my loved one and I thought through the funeral?

- Have I written an obituary and maybe a eulogy?

PRAYER:

Jesus, You are God, so You didn't have to prepare spiritually, and Your mother certainly didn't have to prepare a will. But as You journeyed to Calvary, You told the holy women of Jerusalem to weep, not for You, but for their children – in other words, to prepare. And even as You were dying on the cross, You took the time to give Your mother to Your Apostle, John. As we prepare for the possibility of losing our loved one, help us to focus on what is truly important. In Jesus' Name we pray. Amen.

**Our Lady of Good Remedy,
pray for us.**

✝

Chapter 15

Alternative Medicine, Clinical Trials, and Other Last-Ditch Efforts

"And after you have suffered a little while, the God of all grace, who has called you to his eternal glory in Christ, will himself restore, establish, and strengthen you."
- 1 Peter 5:10 (RSVCE)

There are plenty of books with in-depth discussions about alternative medicine and people more qualified than I am to discuss it. However, you will discover that lots of people are going to offer you suggestions about natural alternatives, and, if you are sick enough, you are likely to be offered the opportunity to participate in a clinical trial.

Here, I just want to share what we personally found helpful and what we did not, as well as some things to consider when you have to make life and death decisions in uncertain circumstances – something that happens more often than not.

As I've mentioned before, Stu lived eight years after his initial cancer diagnosis. In addition to prayer and traditional medicine, I believe that eating organic food and cutting out sugar to make his system as alkaline as possible helped. To save money, we began buying organic vegetables from a local food cooperative, which was something new to me.

After my sister was diagnosed with cancer, she began a radically healthy eating plan, and her cancer appeared to go into remission for a year, a wonderful year which she joyfully spent with her family. But it then came back with a vengeance.

So, in these two cases, eating healthy helped, but did not cure my loved ones.

Other treatments – both natural and medical – did the opposite. It's scary when you're making life and death decisions without all the facts. But as patients reach the end of the road, they are often willing to try things they wouldn't have considered before.

We believe one alternative medicine was key to extending Stu's life. We also tried something developed by a doctor who formerly worked at a large cancer hospital. However, we believe that interfered with that alternative medicine, to Stu's detriment.

We had one scary incident in which Stu rubbed his leg with an alternative cream that promised to heal his leg from its cancerous sores. Unfortunately, it did nothing of the sort. Stu was used to living with pain, but normally his pain was constant, which he found bearable. This cream caused shooting pains that had no predictable pattern. At one point, my strong husband started to cry. He said, "I can't stand it."

Once again, God was there. I suggested in an earlier chapter that you put together a medicine closet so that all the medicines that you have lying around the house end up in one place. I had just done that the weekend before this incident occurred. As I took the medicine out of boxes and placed them on the shelves I had placed in the closet, I remembered being surprised to find that we still had tubes of prescription lidocaine, a numbing agent.

When Stu started to cry, I got frantic. My husband didn't cry. I knew he had to be in a lot of pain. I instantly said: "Honey, lidocaine!"

He said, "No, that won't work." He tried soaking his leg, and it didn't help.

I said again: "Lidocaine!"

He still refused. I can't remember all that happened in the next few minutes, but finally I said one more time: "LIDOCAINE!"

This time he said: "OKAY!"

I ran upstairs to get it, came down, put on my gloves, and slathered it all over his leg. The relief was instant!

I still remember him sitting in the living room afterwards eating a nice dinner and greeting me with a big smile on his face.

"Thank you," he said sheepishly.

No! Thank YOU, God, for inspiring me to make up that medicine closet just before we really needed it.

Lesson Learned: Put all of your medicines in one place where you can easily find them. You never know what you might need. After this incident, we went to our primary care doctor who was happy to provide Stu with a refillable prescription for lidocaine, which helped tremendously with his pain.

Lesson Learned: If you're going to try an unknown remedy, start slowly and small. Instead of slathering a cream on your whole leg, for example, dab it on a tiny spot. See what happens.

Clinical Trials

Although clinical trials are conducted by medical doctors, there's a reason they are called trials. If you are offered such a trial, please read the side effects and the statistical results very closely. Sometimes the side effects are so bad, you wouldn't want the extra few weeks or months they might give you (and often that little bit of time is all that is promised). Other times, the chances of them working are slim to none. The Catholic Church does not require – or prevent – you from engaging in "extraordinary measures."

After Stu's initial diagnosis, we went to another top hospital in Pennsylvania. They told us about a drug which Stu would have had to take for something like three years, which had a 1% chance – 1% – of helping him, but which had terrible side effects. We instantly decided against it. However, when I expressed my disbelief that anyone would take such a drug, I was told that there are people who say yes to this.

This was at the beginning of our journey. I know now that these people were undoubtedly at the end of their journey and felt they had no other choice but to try this drug.

Clinical trials are important, and someone has to be the guinea pig. Medical breakthroughs happen every day. That is what Stu and I (as so many before us) hoped would happen before he died. In this area, however, each of us must forge our own path.

Stu's leukemia was cured by drugs that, at one time, must have gone through the experimental process. When offered a drug as part of a clinical trial, you might want to ask what stage of the three-stage process the drug is in. Both my husband and my sister would submit to an experimental drug when they ran out of other options. In both these cases, the drug, at best, did not work; at worst, I believe it hastened their deaths.

Lesson Learned: Make sure you truly understand the side effects of any experimental drug, the likelihood for success, and how success is defined. Are we talking about a few more weeks of life? A few more months? A year? When other options are gone, patients often take big risks. Make sure you really think through whether or not the risk is worth taking.

Last-Ditch Efforts

Over the rest of 2010 and 2011, Stu and I did a variety of things to try to extend his life. We traveled to H. Lee Moffitt Cancer Center in Tampa to see if Stu was eligible for something called an isolated limb perfusion. The doctor there was extraordinarily kind, but Stu wasn't a candidate.

We faced various emergencies. One Sunday, I left Stu at home with a home health aide to go to a church that we joined when I first got to EWTN, and we were living behind the Network. We stayed with it even after we bought our home in another part of town.

After Communion, I remember looking at my phone and seeing a text telling me that Stu had a heart incident and was being transported to a local hospital. I got in my car and drove frantically to the hospital. It wasn't a hospital I was super familiar with, so I had to drive around the campus trying to find the correct building, and then walk around trying to find the correct end of the building, and then the correct room.

Once I arrived, Stu took my hand and said: "Don't worry honey. I wasn't going anywhere without you." He knew I would take the long way to the hospital – not because I wanted to, but because I am directionally challenged and didn't know the shortest way to get from that side of town to the hospital.

Events like that were common in our lives at that point. In fact, at this point, emergencies were more the norm than the exception. But I was grateful for the time we had. Being by my husband's side was always comforting, and he was always interesting to me.

During this time, Stu also found a wonderful doctor who performed a number of surgeries on Stu, not to cure him, but to help him live more comfortably with his cancer-riddled leg.

You might think things were pretty grim at this point – and medically, they were. But as I was soon to discover, Stu had one last hurrah in him.

REFLECTION QUESTIONS

- When I am offered a clinical trial, what is my plan for evaluating this option? Does it include God? If you're not sure if what is being offered is ethical, contact The National Catholic Bioethics Center (NCBC) in Broomall, Pennsylvania, www.ncbcenter.org. You can not only ask an NCBC ethicist for guidance in moral decision-making online, but, in emergency situations, you can even call 215-877-2660 anytime day or night and someone will help you. The website itself is also a treasure trove of information.

- How do my loved one and I define "success," and does our idea of success line up with the success being offered by the clinical trial I am considering?

PRAYER:

Dear Jesus, while on the cross, You accepted the wine flavored with vinegar, but not the wine flavored with myrrh. When faced with making life-or-death decisions about using unproven and experimental drugs, please help us to rest in the knowledge that You are the one who brought us into being and You are the one who will decide when we die. Please grant us the grace to weigh the pros and cons of these impossible decisions, and to find peace in knowing that You love us more than we love ourselves. Help us to trust that, when we unite ourselves with You on the Cross, You will help us to make the best decision possible for us, even if that means we must suffer "a little while." In Jesus' name we pray. Amen.

Our Lady of Perpetual Help, pray for us.

STATION OF THE CROSS:
Jesus Meets the Women of Jerusalem

The holy women of Jerusalem wept when they saw what was happening to their Lord. In the face of both indifference and cruelty, their caring and their prayers must have been a balm to the wounded Heart of Our Savior. During our travels, we will meet people who will go out of their way to make our journey special. They may never know how much their kindness meant to us, but You know, Lord. You know. May they be richly blessed!

Chapter 16:

The How and Why of Traveling with a Seriously Ill Loved One

"I lift up my eyes to the hills. From whence does my help come?
My help comes from the LORD, who made heaven and earth."
- Psalm 121:1-2 (RSVCE)

I remember walking in the door one evening to find my terminally ill husband sitting at our computer. We didn't know it at the time, but he had less than a year to live. As I walked into the house, Stu gave me a look of complete joy as he pronounced, "I've figured out where we're going to go on vacation this year."

A million thoughts raced through my mind at that moment. Fortunately, I kept them to myself.

"You did?" I managed to say. "Where?"

"A dude ranch in Wyoming," he said enthusiastically. "I found a ranch that looks really great, and I've been on the phone with the owners. It's perfect." He gestured toward the computer screen. "Take a look!"

As I walked over to the screen, my emotions were as jumbled as my thoughts. Understand, neither of us rode horses. How would he get his cancerous leg, which was easily three times the size of his normal leg, over a horse? Would we be able to bring all the bandages we would need to wrap and rewrap his leg? What kind of fun could he have with the cancer sucking so much of his energy out of him?

But even as those thoughts swirled inside my head, I was – thanks be to God – keenly aware that this was the most excited Stu had been in, well, *years*. He was animated, engaged, and happy. So, on top of all those thoughts came the one that I'm sure was inspired by God: If he dies doing this, at least he'll die happy.

"Okay," I said.

He looked thrilled. "Okay? We'll go?"

"Let's do it!"

Thank God, thank God, *thank God*, I said yes. You'll understand why in a minute. But first, I want to say this:

A lot of people think that when someone has a terminal illness – or they have been impaired by a series of strokes or other medical conditions – that this limits them to staying home and going to visit the doctor. While an illness can progress to that stage, it's important that the people supporting a loved one respect them enough to allow them to continue to live life on their own terms, to let them decide when they have reached that stage, and, most importantly, when they haven't.

This doesn't mean it's going to be easy, but with the right attitude, you will be surprised how meaningful such a trip can be, the memories it makes, and how happy you will be that you acted like a spouse instead of a parent to your loved one. This latter point is so important. I will make it again and again.

I will tell you; I was nervous – and not just about the medical logistics. My prior equestrian experience consisted of a pony ride at a local fair as a kid. Stu didn't have a lot of experience, either. Plus, a dude ranch? Just how rustic was this going to be? I am decidedly not Jane, Queen of the Jungle! But I pushed those thoughts aside, and, when thoughts of falling off a horse and getting paralyzed occurred (yes, really), I gave those thoughts to God.

My husband had a wonderful time figuring out how we were going to get to Wyoming. Should we drive or fly? (At this point, we felt his leg was as big as it was going to get so why not fly?) What did we need to bring on the trip? How long could we afford to be gone?

I remember going to a tack shop, which (for neophytes like I was) is a store that sells equestrian goods. The ranch required that guests wear boots. Could we find one large enough to fit over Stu's cancerous lower leg? The shop had to send away for boots big enough to fit him, but we got them! So, off we went.

We encountered numerous obstacles on our trip out west. At the time, there were no direct flights from Birmingham to Jackson Hole, so we had to fly into Denver. But, as luck would have it, our flight into Jackson Hole was cancelled. Gulp. I remember setting Stu up in the airport, bringing him a drink and a snack, and then running around the airport and eventually ending up in a long line to see about alternate flights.

Unfortunately, there were no other flights into Jackson Hole that day, so we had to spend the night. This was a disaster because all of Stu's medical supplies were in his checked bag, which was unavailable.

Lesson Learned: Pay for an additional carry-on bag if necessary, but always carry your medical supplies with you.

We took a cab to the nearest hotel. I was going to ask the cab driver to take us to a drug store first, but we only had a few hours to get some sleep, so my husband, who was decidedly not a prima donna, nixed that idea. We went straight to a hotel and slept in our clothes.

Although we called the hotel in Jackson Hole the night before to inform them that we would be late, the night clerk apparently didn't inform the day clerk because, when we arrived in our rental car, we discovered that the clerk was just about give away our room – the last room in the hotel!

Lesson Learned: If there is likely to be shift change at the hotel to which you are traveling, call both shifts

Thank God we got that room. Because he was unable to change his bandages, Stu was a mess. He took a shower, and I bandaged his leg; then he took a nap while I explored Jackson Hole on foot. There was a wonderful outdoor art festival going on, and I had the opportunity to enjoy lots of local art, including some paintings of the area, which is absolutely gorgeous. It made me eager to get a glimpse of the real-life wonders depicted in the paintings.

We had a nice dinner at a local restaurant that evening and retired early. The next day, we got on the road to The Lazy L&B Ranch in Dubois, Wyoming, which is about a two-and-a-half-hour drive from Jackson Hole. The scenery was beautiful, but as we got further and further from town, my trepidation increased – especially when we turned off the highway and onto a dirt road! I said nothing, but I did wonder what exactly we had gotten ourselves into.

When the ranch finally popped into view, I breathed a huge sigh of relief! Below us, nestled in a gorgeous valley, sat the ranch, and it looked *amazing*. We would discover that this area is known as the Wind River Valley, and indeed the Wind River ran through the ranch. You could actually hear it. The ranch was surrounded by mountains on three sides – if I'm remembering correctly, three different mountain ranges. It was spectacular! So, some days, when Stu needed to rest, I would hike up from the valley to the main road, saying my prayers and reveling in all that mountain grandeur.

We drove into the ranch, were assigned our cabin and our horses for the week, and took an introductory ride around the ranch. Could Stu get up on a horse with that leg? With a step stool, he managed. We didn't go far, and we didn't go fast, but we did ride that day. Mission accomplished!

That night, we ate in the log cabin with the rest of the group. Everyone was extremely friendly, especially the woman who owned the ranch at the time. The next morning, we were up early. The first ride took us up, up, up a mountain. As we crested the top, it reminded me of the opening scene in *The Sound of Music*, where Julie Andrews opens her arms and runs around the mountain meadow singing, "The hills are alive with the sound of music." You'll be happy to know I refrained from doing the same – but I wanted to!

So, I was pretty happy about getting up the mountain. However, for me, going down was a bit more (read "a lot more") scary – beautiful, but scary. The slant was so steep, I wondered if I was going to remain seated! Did I mention I am somewhat afraid of heights? I decided to trust my horse – and the Lord! My terminally ill husband, however, who had been extremely athletic his entire life, was loving it. So, for that reason, I felt happy that we had made this journey.

Back at the ranch, we ate lunch with everyone else, and Stu retired to our cabin for a nap. I was happy to forego the afternoon ride and explore the ranch, read, and just relax. We enjoyed dinner with the group that night and prepared to ride the next day.

To be honest, we didn't make any more of the hours-long rides, and we missed things like the town rodeo and the square dance. Stu wasn't up to it. But thanks to the caring ranch owner, we still had an incredible time.

We did enjoy one private ride of maybe two hours along the (flat) Wind River and through the countryside. I had another ride by myself, and, for the first time in my life, did target practice with a real gun. Yikes!

But the two of us also took a day to drive into the town of Dubois where we went to the National Bighorn Sheep Interpretive Center, which was a real treat! We ate at a local restaurant and picked up a paper which talked about range wars, and other topics we thought only existed in the movies.

Another day we went to shop in town and purchased some local items like a bracelet and photos of the glory that surrounded us! Stu couldn't hike, but the ranch owner also told us about an incredible drive we could take through the mountains, where we stopped at various scenic points and enjoyed the outdoors.

One memorable day, the ranch owner took us on a ride in her jeep where she pointed out all kinds of flowers and other local vegetation, which we wouldn't have noticed on our own. We ended up at the place where the entire group was enjoying a chuck wagon dinner. They had put out two camp chairs just for us because Stu couldn't sit on the ground with that leg, and they brought the dinner to us. It was such an incredibly thoughtful thing to do. Stu was thrilled.

The final night, there was a dinner around the campfire. Stu wasn't up to going, but he insisted that I go because, as he said, I had to eat. Everyone told stories about what they most enjoyed about the week. At the end, the ranch owners gave Stu and me a coffee table book, filled with photos of the ranches in the area, including The Lazy L&B. Everyone, including the entire staff, had signed the book, many expressing what an inspiration my husband was to them. One man even gave us a pair of moose antlers he had found – and we actually managed to bring them back to Alabama!

Everyone had to leave early the next morning, but the owner told us to stay as long as we needed to. The ranch manager even met us at our hotel back in Jackson Hole. We went to a local restaurant for lunch and then she took us around Yellowstone in her jeep. In addition to the incredible scenery, which included spectacular waterfalls, we saw and got relatively close to several moose!

It was a vacation that no one could have predicted. It was the ranch owner, the ranch manager, and the kindness of strangers in the group, which made the trip so memorable. Stu would say to me later that he wanted to take that trip because he knew I would never do it myself. He was absolutely right. Left to my own devices, I would NEVER have taken a trip like that. I only did it for him. But sick as he was, we ended up having the time of our lives. As Stu said, time and time again, "Honey, I can be sick anywhere."

Lesson Learned: Make the effort to have fun. Even if you can't do everything, there are likely to be surprises that will lift the heaviness of the diagnosis and provide memories of a lifetime.

But there was one more lesson to be learned, and this one wasn't pretty. That night in the hotel room, Stu was in the bathroom when I heard him yell out: "OH, GROSS!"

My heart sank. I was sitting on the hotel bed, and I remember steeling myself for whatever was to come. I croaked out: "What's wrong, honey?"

He was right. What he was about to say was beyond gross. The ranch obviously had lots of horses — and horses attract flies. Probably while he was sleeping, at least one of them had gotten beneath the bandages around his leg and laid eggs in one of his wounds. Yes, he had maggots.

I thought I would die. I remember wrapping my arms around myself, bending over in the bed, and quickly saying: "Jesus, PLEASE, help Stu to figure out a way to be okay with this." I have no idea why that was my prayer, but it was.

A few minutes later, Stu exited the bathroom. "You know what?" he said. "In the past, they used maggots to clean wounds, so it's okay."

Prayer answered! Of course, we had to get those maggots out, and we did. Well, I did – with a pair of tweezers. But the Divine

Physician helped me with that, too. So, yes, there were moments that were hard and yucky, to say the least, and things we couldn't do, but the good obviously outweighed the bad, and, if I had to do it again, I would – in a heartbeat!

Lesson Learned: Don't forget to meet the hard moments with a quick prayer! God is there!

Our Wyoming adventure obviously stands out, but as I've tried to show you throughout this book, that wasn't the only "break" we took over the eight years Stu was sick. I share these stories to encourage you to find some fun in the midst of things that are decidedly not fun.

I thank God we decided to take this trip because the hardest times were yet to come.

Lesson Learned: Your life isn't over until it's over. Every day is a gift; make the most of it!

REFLECTION QUESTIONS:

- What can I do to help make the most of the time I still have with my loved one – even if what we decide to do doesn't make "sense" to anyone but my loved one and me?

- If my loved one is still of sound mind (or even retains some capacity to reason), how can I encourage them to make their own decisions as they are able, with me as a support and sounding board?

PRAYER:

Dear Jesus, thank You for showing me how to support my loved one's dreams as he/she potentially reaches the end of his/her earthly life. Thank You for sending holy people who help us, not just in bad times, but in the good times, and with the good memories that are still ours to make! Thank You for all the times You help us find calm in the midst of a storm. Help us to know we can still use the gifts You have given us to bring joy not only to each other, but to those You put in our path. In Jesus' name we pray. Amen.

**Mary, Cause of Our Joy,
pray for us.**

STATION OF THE CROSS:
Jesus is Stripped of His Garments

The Roman soldiers weren't satisfied with merely torturing Jesus. They also wanted to humiliate Him by stripping Him naked before the world. When a loved one is seriously ill, they are slowly stripped of many things that are important to them. Some of them are small things, like the indignity of having someone help with toileting. Some of them are large, like having a leg amputated. Help us Lord, to face these indignities like You did – with courage, and strength, and with humility, which is the foundation of all virtues.

Chapter 17

Amputation

"And a sword will pierce through your own soul also."
- Luke 2:35 (RSVCE)

Of all the things that happened to us during Stu's three bouts with cancer, one of the hardest for me was the day he decided that the only option left for him was to have his leg amputated – up to the hip.

After talking this over with his doctor, my husband was actually happy about this decision. He was tired of dragging his smelly, lymph leaking, gigantic leg around. He thought it would give him a new lease on life.

I can't be sure, because my husband could read me pretty well, but I think I managed to swallow my fear while I was around him. But, alone in the car, on my way home from the hospital, I called my mother to give her the news. I could hardly talk.

Finally, I just burst out: "Mom, I'm so scared."

She said, "Honey, what are you afraid of?"

I paused a moment. Finally, I said: "I don't understand how he's going to be able to sit!"

As soon as those words left my mouth, I felt a lot of the terror that was bottled up inside me start to ebb away. Sharing the burden with a person who loved me, and who I knew wasn't judging me, lightened it.

I know that's true for others as well. Years earlier, Stu and I stopped to talk to a friend after a church service. We knew her husband had developed a problem with hiccups. He couldn't stop, and it had gotten very serious. As we talked and explored different options, she said: "Talking to you doesn't make it seem so bad."

The trick is finding the right person with whom to share your fear. Shortly after Stu was diagnosed with his first bout of melanoma, a woman came up to me after church – hear this – after church. She said she had heard Stu had cancer and wanted to know more about it. I didn't know her that well, but I was still new at this, so I gave her the basics. Unbelievably, this is what she said: "I knew a man who had melanoma once…he died."

Lesson Learned: If you can, find someone with whom to share your deepest fears. It helps to say things out loud. It helps you to clarify why you are afraid. A burden shared – *but only with the right person* – is a burden lessened.

Lesson Learned: How do you find a person in whom you can confide? You may be fortunate enough to have a family member or friend with whom you can share everything. But if not, understand that not all friends are able or willing to be helpful in every circumstance. For example, a friend whose husband is an architect or a carpenter might help you figure out who to call if you need to retrofit your house for a disability, but not so helpful when it comes to sharing your fears about an upcoming procedure. Think through everyone you encounter on a daily basis and find out if they have had an experience similar to yours. Then test the waters and see if they are willing to discuss it.

Lesson Learned: Sometimes people say terrible things to you. As Mother Teresa said in her famous poem, "Forgive them." Or, as Jesus said, "Father, forgive them, for they know not what they do." I would also say that it helps to share that burden with a person of faith, although, as the previous story illustrates, don't be too quick to share until you know at least a little of that person's heart.

Because my family and Stu's remaining family were up in Virginia, and we were in Alabama, we were most often alone in coping with our situation. I know having only each other to lean on helped us grow together as a couple, so, in general, it was a blessing. However, in the case of this amputation, I really didn't want to be alone. Fortunately, Stu's sister flew down for the operation, for which I was grateful.

You might think that the night before the amputation the atmosphere in our home would have been filled with fear, but my husband actually joked about it. He said he was going to do a YouTube video showing him with both legs one day and then the next day looking down at himself without a leg and screaming "Ahhh...my leg! Where did it go? The aliens took it!" So silly, but it relieved the pressure. He also joked about the loss of his smelly leg being a relief to "nostrils around the world."

But that levity didn't mean the surgery itself didn't scare him. I remember the day of the surgery like it was yesterday. We waited the entire day for doctors to operate. That meant no eating or drinking for my poor husband as we waited and waited for the dreaded moment.

Stu did know that after the surgery he would be intubated. He told me he had a terrible gag reflex, so he made me promise I would tell the doctors to keep him asleep until it could be removed.

Stu was finally called back into the waiting area to be prepped. I was allowed to be with him. We waited and waited – and then, the orderlies came. It turned out Stu was the last surgery of the day.

We kissed goodbye. I remember watching my incredible husband sitting up in his hospital bed as the orderlies began wheeling the bed towards the operating room. His hands gripped the sides of the hospital bed. He turned his head away from me and towards the operating room. I watched him as he straightened up as much as possible in the bed, and like a soldier going into battle; he gave a curt nod toward the room. It was the bravest thing I've ever seen.

He would tell me later that they had laid the saw (yes, the saw) they were going to use on the operating table so he could see it. I think I would have fainted right there. But he didn't.

The surgery took hours. It was very late at night when they finally came to tell me the surgery had been completed and it was "successful." My sister-in-law and I moved from the waiting room to a recovery area.

When they allowed me into the recovery room, I could hardly believe what I was seeing. There were tubes everywhere. I couldn't see the surgical site, but I saw all the machines around him that were keeping him stable.

The doctor told me that they were able to keep more of the leg than they thought. That turned out to be wrong, but I remember whispering that to Stu even though he was still appeared to be out of it. However, as I stood there, he began to stir, probably because he heard my voice, and he immediately started to gag. I flew around the room, grabbed the doctor, and said, "Put him back to sleep! Please…put him back to sleep! He can't be awake while he is intubated!" Fortunately, the doctor listened to me, and Stu quickly went back to sleep.

However, the next day he would remember what I had told him about having more of his leg than they thought. It was amazing to me that my voice could get through to him even in his postoperative fugue state.

My sister-in-law and I went home in the wee hours of the morning and grabbed a few hours of sleep. As we entered the room later that morning, I had no idea what to expect. Would he be in pain? Depressed? Scared?

I needn't have worried. My incredible husband was, as usual, entertaining the doctors and nurses. No one could believe that a man who had just had his leg sawed off could be so happy. But because all that cancer had been taken off his body, Stu's energy level began to soar. He felt better than he had in a long time.

The hospital staff immediately got Stu up and out of bed so he could learn how to maneuver on one leg. It wouldn't be long before he would transition from the surgical unit to a rehabilitation unit.

The question was: Should he stay at University of Alabama Birmingham (UAB) or move to Lakeshore Rehabilitation Hospital, which is a training center for the U.S. Olympic and Paralympic teams? My sister-in-law and I visited both. We decided to keep Stu in the same hospital for his initial rehabilitation. He would have follow-up therapy at Lakeshore.

Stu had always been an athlete. When he transitioned to the rehab center at UAB, he told his physical therapists that he wanted to get a manual wheelchair so he could work his upper body. I was skeptical. Fortunately, one of the UAB doctors took an interest in him.

He said to him, "Stu, this is the best you're ever going to be. This is probably the one shot you have of getting a wheelchair from your insurance company. You've got to go for an electric wheelchair now." That made sense to my husband, so that is what he did.

Thank God he did, as you will see later.

Lesson Learned: Always go for the best equipment you can get.

Retrofitting the House

As Stu was getting rehabilitated, I learned that the hospital wouldn't discharge him until he had a safe place to go. It would have been helpful if someone had brought this to our attention pre-surgery, but whose job would that be? The surgeons are only concerned about the operation. No one was thinking about what would happen after the operation – including us.

I asked about places that had the kind of equipment we would need. They referred me to a local store, which had an amazing array of items as well as several handicapped bathroom displays. The store was connected to a man who drew up the plans, and to a contractor, who carried them out.

Exactly what kinds of things do you need when retrofitting your home? We needed a ramp to go from the garage into the kitchen. The bump on the floor under the door needed little mini-ramps on either side so the wheelchair could roll up from the garage and down into the kitchen. The island in the kitchen, which I discovered had been bolted to the floor, had to be moved to the wall. Doorways had to be widened throughout the main level. The toilet in the powder room had to be made ADA-compliant, with grab bars on either side.

Fortunately, our master bedroom was on the main floor. The biggest change was to the master bathroom, which had to be almost completely gutted. Out with the toilet closet and the jetted tub. In with the roll-in shower and a lowered sink under which the wheelchair could fit as well as an accordion mirror that Stu could use for shaving.

Stu approved the design, with changes. For example, he wanted to be able to turn on the shower while still outside the shower, so the water could warm up before he wheeled himself in. Smart! He also wanted a showerhead over the shower seat as well as coming out from the wall in front of him.

I too had a thousand decisions to make. What tile should we use in the bathroom? What color should we paint the walls? What style of faucet should he have? Was it okay to use the sink the contractor had on hand, which would save us money, or did we want a new one?

Usually, these kinds of decisions take me forever to make. But I didn't have forever. I prayed that God would help me make good decisions, and He did. I picked a paint to go with the tile that the man who helped design the bathroom didn't especially like. But after it was on, the painters gushed about how good it looked. Thank you, Lord!

The whole thing was accomplished in about two weeks – which is pretty unbelievable – and Stu was discharged.

Lesson Learned: Does God care about the color we paint our bathroom? If we ask Him to, He does! How good it is to know we are not alone!

The New Normal

The time immediately after the operation was pretty good. We were fortunate enough to be living a reasonable distance from Lakeshore. We purchased a van with a ramp, so Stu could drive his wheelchair up the ramp, and then transfer from his wheelchair to the driver's seat, which rotated towards the back. It was a little harder than it looked to drive up the ramp, and, at one point Stu fell off the ramp in his wheelchair while outside of Lakeshore. But Stu was a tough guy. He managed to right himself and his wheelchair and get on with his workout.

My husband especially loved swimming (they had a seat outside the pool that lowered him down into the pool) and floor volleyball. While Stu swam, he loved to say the Chaplet of Divine Mercy, over and over again. How much that must have pleased Our Lord!

Things were settling into a new normal, but it was not to last.

REFLECTION QUESTIONS:

- If my loved one is facing a potentially life-altering procedure, have I thought through what alternations I may need to make at home so that he or she can be comfortable and able to maintain as much independence as possible?

- What have I done to help myself forgive those who say hurtful or even cruel things to me during this time? Who might I have inadvertently hurt in my own life?

PRAYER:

Blessed Mother, you did not stand at the foot of the cross alone. You were able to lean upon three other Mary's as well as the Apostle John, whom Jesus gives you as your son. Help me to picture myself standing with you under your Son's Cross. Then, hold my hand dear Mother, as you and I stand together at the foot of my loved one's cross. Jesus, even as I take Your hand and the hand of Your mother, I ask You to please send me family and friends who are still here on earth, just as You sent the Apostle John to support Your mother. But, if not, as the three of us stand together at the foot of the cross, help me to know, deep in my heart, that with You and Your Mother – and all my saint friends – I am never really alone.

Our Lady of Mount Carmel, Most Tender Mother, pray for us.

STATION OF THE CROSS:
Jesus is Nailed to the Cross

Jesus is nailed naked to a tree. There is no turning back. It is only a matter of time until He dies. But despite this, Jesus spends His time giving His mother a home with the Apostle John ("Woman, behold they son. Behold, thy mother"), forgiving his persecutors ("Father, forgive them, for they know not what they do"), bringing the "Good Thief" to paradise ("Today you will be with Me in paradise"), drinking the cup His Father has given Him to the last drop ("I thirst...It is finished...Father, into Thy hands, I commend my spirit."). And He is not alone. Mary, his mother, stands at the foot of the Cross, along with Salome, Mary's sister; Mary, wife of Clopas; Mary Magdalene, and the Apostle John. Thankfully, the caregiver finds loved ones and friends who will begin to gather around, if they haven't already, to help shoulder the load. And while the caregiver suspects the end may be near, he or she knows, just as Jesus knew, there is still more to be done physically, and, most especially, spiritually.

Chapter 18

Paralysis

But rejoice insofar as you are sharing Christ's sufferings,
so that you may also be glad and shout for joy
when his glory is revealed."
- 1 Peter 4:13 (RSVCE)

I think most people probably have one thing of which they are most afraid. We never spoke of this during his illness, but I knew from a talk we had years ago that the one thing Stu was most afraid of was becoming paralyzed. Unfortunately, that is what began to happen.

All of a sudden, Stu started to lose feeling in his arm and hand. He tried to shake it off, but it got worse, and worse, and worse. Soon, Stu couldn't lift himself out of his wheelchair. He was terrified. What was happening? How could this be?

I took my husband in for an outpatient MRI. It was in that office that I first saw a flyer for a home healthcare agency. I had no idea these places even existed, but I was getting worried because my husband was a big a man and I knew that I couldn't lift him. I needed to investigate my options.

Fortunately, I have a family that loves me. When the time came, they would all contribute what they could to this healthcare challenge. My mother and my sisters were on the phone with me every day and sent me money when they could. When my brother Larry heard what was happening, he called me and said, "Chelle, don't use your retirement money for this. I will pay for home healthcare." I can't even tell you what a blessing this was. (If you need financial help, please turn to the "Resources" section of this book.)

Stu's Paralysis Worsens

I took my husband to see a number of doctors, but no one wanted to touch him. We finally ended up in a surgeon's office. We knew this doctor was our last resort.

I remember wheeling Stu in and bending over the back of his wheelchair to hug him. He was in despair. Once again, my heart was breaking. Would this doctor help us?

Miraculously, the answer was yes. This was a young, hotshot surgeon who said the problem was in Stu's neck and that he had performed many such surgeries with great success. We were elated.

Stu had the operation, which did indeed appear to be a success. We were told Stu would need physical therapy to regain his movement, but that everything would be okay. It's hard to express how relieved we were.

Special Conversation

The day after the surgery, Stu and I had a beautiful day in the atrium of the hospital. For some reason, we were the only ones there. At that point, my husband and I had been married 34 years. By that time, most couples think they've heard each other's stories. But he surprised me!

Stu began to talk about being on board a Navy warship. These were stories I had never heard, perhaps a) because many things were classified back then, b) because he didn't want to worry me about what could happen, or, most likely, c) because my husband was a humble man. However, by the time of this conversation, Stu's ship had long since been decommissioned, and this was just the right time to look back over our lives and share.

That afternoon, I learned that my husband had disarmed a sailor aboard that ship who had gone a little crazy, thus preventing things from going very badly for the young man.

I also learned about the night he was up on the quarterdeck with the Captain of the ship. My husband had grown up around boats, so he was very savvy. His ship, along with a number of others, was protecting an aircraft carrier in the middle of the ocean.

Okay, I'm going to use civilian language here. Believe me, I'm paraphrasing here and may be getting the details wrong, but this was the gist of his story.

The aircraft carrier put out a message that it was turning right (starboard) and the fleet surrounding the carrier started to follow. Stu looked closely at the situation and said, "Captain, that carrier is not turning away from us. It's coming right at us." The Captain said, "Are you sure?" Stu assured him he was. The Captain radioed the carrier. (Okay, this is the salty part of the book.) "WTF?" It turned out that the carrier was indeed turning toward the warships and that call diverted a disaster. My husband was a hero, and I had never even known it!

That was a happy day, and Stu was feeling optimistic.

Our Biggest Mistake

Our surgeon, like most hospital workers, really liked Stu. He was a likeable guy! Before I returned the next day, Stu had a talk with his surgeon. When I got to Stu's room, he asked me to stop by the doctor's office.

I was a little confused, but I went. The surgeon told me that Stu had an amazing attitude, which I knew, and that he was certain he could do the necessary rehabilitation exercises – at home! It turned out that Stu had asked the surgeon to talk to me because he knew I wouldn't think this was a good idea. He was right.

I argued. The surgeon pushed back, implying this was going to be very simple.

Finally, I said, "Well, what if it doesn't work?"

He said, "Then you just come back."

I looked him in the eye. "So, you're saying if it doesn't work, we can come back to the hospital?"

"Of course," he said.

I believed him.

Big mistake.

Stu was jubilant about coming home. He started to work on the exercises, but he quickly discovered it was harder than he thought. Actually, it was impossible. He started to get worried.

I called to get him back into Trinity Hospital. Oh no, we were told. Once you are discharged, you can't come back. But, but, but... I also tried local physical therapists but none of them had the facilities to help someone as disabled as my husband.

Stu was in despair. He looked at me and said: "I've ruined my life."

I flashed back to the memory of working in the Archdiocese of Philadelphia. While there, I had a young man working for me whose sister had fallen off the back deck of her house and broken her neck. She had just cancelled her insurance for monetary reasons. If she had gotten rehab, she would almost assuredly have been okay. But the state of Mississippi, which is where she lived, did not provide this kind of help for residents and so she became a quadriplegic.

If it was in my power to do so, I was not going to let this happen to my husband!

Lesson Learned: Never, ever, *ever* leave the hospital until everything is taken care of. Don't believe you can return. Doctors do not always know what's possible procedurally, even at their own hospital. Every hospital has a "patient advocate." If you're told something like this, ask the patient advocate if it's true.

I Prayed; God Answered

Until this time, I thought the amputation was the most stressful time in Stu's illness. But this surpassed even that. I knew I was all Stu had. I had to come through for him. I called everyone I could think of: doctors, physical therapists, and our insurance company. Finally, I decided to go in person to the office of the surgeon who had led me astray. Before I left, I got down on my knees and begged the Lord to help me.

I showed up at the office and his nurse was at the front desk. I prevailed upon her to let me talk to the doctor. Just then the doctor walked out and saw me. I could see that if he could have turned around and left without my seeing him, he would have. But because I was standing right in front of him, he had no choice but to talk with me.

I told him I just needed him to write a prescription for my husband to get into Lakeshore. He slowly walked over to the front desk, picked up a pen, and signed the paper. I quietly thanked him and walked outside. Yes! Thank You Lord! I rushed jubilantly back to my car!

Lesson Learned: It's very difficult for someone who is terminally ill to fight for themselves. That's why caregivers are so important. But you, as a caregiver, can only do so much. When things seem impossible, turn to the Lord. He is your only safety.

My husband couldn't believe it. He had hope again. We had hope again.

I called Lakeshore to make the arrangements. But before we left, my husband and I had an argument.

Because Stu could barely move, I wanted our home health aides to be with him in the hospital. Stu thought the hospital nurses would be enough. I couldn't bear to think of him needing to do something like scratch his nose at night and not being able to. I insisted he have 'round the clock care. Thanks to my brother, we could afford it. Finally, Stu gave in. The first day wasn't even over, when Stu looked at me sheepishly, nodded at the home health aide and said, "Thank you." Of course, my love. Of course.

Lakeshore Attempts to Reverse Stu's Paralysis

Lakeshore was an amazing experience. The doctor there did many innovative things. She had me go to a local apothecary, which is a kind of pharmacy where they put together custom drugs, which she gave Stu. The doctors and therapists there did everything they could for Stu, but he never regained his mobility.

My vibrant, beautiful husband had officially become a quadriplegic.

In his final days at Lakeshore, I took Stu outside in a wheelchair so we could have a little picnic, but he was drooping forward in his chair. His precious face was red with a rash – I have no idea why. I could see that not only was the paralysis getting worse, but his fatigue was coming back. Although part of me denied it, I knew in my heart that the cancer was killing him.

We returned home, and I tried to make him as comfortable as possible – until I couldn't.

Lesson Learned: If Stu had not had the opportunity to regain his mobility, I would have always felt like I had failed; that he might have been cured if only I had done a better job. If you want to avoid regrets, it's important to meet every challenge with hope and prayer and with dogged determination – and I am so very grateful to God that I was given the opportunity to do so.

Lesson Learned: As you read the previous chapter on Stu's amputation, you might have been thinking it was a shame Stu didn't have his leg amputated earlier. But by the time that option was mentioned, the cancer had already spread beyond that leg and, as you can now see, the resulting paralysis would almost certainly have overcome him much sooner. God only allowed this suffering for a short while.

REFLECTION QUESTIONS:

- If a doctor tells me something about a hospital procedure that doesn't ring true, do I know to whom I might turn to verify whatever it is I need to know, i.e., a patient advocate, nursing supervisor, insurance company, physical therapist, fellow caregivers, and more?

- What have I done in the past to give myself the courage I need to act when I am afraid? Am I using that knowledge in this situation, or have I given up at the first "no" from a health care professional? Am I prepared to fight for my loved one, if it is necessary, knowing that I am often his or her only hope?

PRAYER:

Jesus, when things seem hopeless, as they did for You on the Cross, help us never to despair. Help us to always remember to turn to You first; to honor You and to give You Glory by knowing in our hearts that, whatever happens, You have the last word. You are with us to deliver us in whatever fashion makes the most sense for our Eternal Salvation – even if that victory occurs on "the other side." Thank you for showing us the way to ultimate victory. Amen.

Our Lady of Sorrows,
pray for us.

✝

Chapter 19

Why Does God Allow Suffering?
A Meditation

"We know that all things work together for good for those who love God, who are called according to his purpose."
- Romans 8:28 (RSVCE)

When things are really bad, it's natural to wonder, at least sometimes, what's going on? Why is this happening? Does God not care? Does He just enjoy testing us? Is all of this just some sort of cosmic joke?

There is an answer to these questions, and it lies in one very important fact, which I recommend you really think about. Our Catholic/Christian faith teaches us that God the Father sent His own Son, His ONLY Son, Jesus Christ, down to earth to suffer and die for you. Yes, you. Even if you were the only person on earth, Jesus would have suffered and died for you.

I often thought about this. If the Father allowed the horrendous torture and death of His own Son, then this is no joke – and surely the Father, whose love is always perfect because God is Love, loves you every bit as much as He loves His own Son.

We know that Jesus died for us. So here's the question: What are *we – you and I –* willing to do for Him? That's the question I asked myself, and it's a question I pose to you.

This is why the Catholic Church, in her wisdom, has Catholics meditate so often on the suffering and death of Jesus – especially during Lent. It's not because the Church wants us all to be sadists who enjoy contemplating suffering and death. It's because most of us – I want to say all of us – are going to encounter some type of suffering in this life and, when we do, she wants to give us a perfect example of how to handle it.

Jesus was true God and true Man. You can see that in this perfect prayer, one that is a model for caregivers: *"My Father, if it be possible, let this cup pass from me; nevertheless, not as I will, but as thou wilt."* - Matthew 26:39 (RSVCE)

These are the words we are invited to pray when it all seems too much! Give it to God and He WILL give you the grace to endure "a little while." Until what? Until we come to ETERNAL REST, where there is no more sorrow, when God will wipe away every tear. Where there is eternal gladness.

KNOW that this is true. Know it with every fiber of your being. Whenever you are tempted to bitterness, counter it with these thoughts. Immerse yourself in them.

And remember, suffering can also take us off the road to perdition – or at least lessen our time in purgatory – and place us on the much more difficult road to sanctity. Eternal Life is something worth suffering for!

Maranatha: Come, Lord Jesus!

Another Fruit of Suffering

Did you know that when people work together to achieve a common goal there is less infighting, more camaraderie, and the job gets done quicker and better? I remember reading about how amazing it was to work at NASA when they were getting ready for the first moon launch. We also know that soldiers who have gone through battle together learn to trust each other, and will often die for each other. The Marines are famous for saying: "Leave no man behind!"

When you, as a couple, make the decision to work together to try to save or at least extend the life of your loved one, I promise you, your marriage WILL get stronger. Your love WILL grow. You WILL become a better person.

I know this is true. You will trust each other more. You will depend on each other more. If the two of you did not become one before, you will now. As a caregiver, you will learn what love really is. Make the decision not to leave your loved one behind!

This is war, and each day is a battle. Fight! I pray this book is showing you how!

REFLECTION QUESTIONS:

Read Psalm 22, in which Jesus cries out: *"My God, My God, why hast Thou forsaken Me?"* (Psalm 22:1) (RSVCE). Many people think that this is a cry of despair, but if you read the entire Psalm, you will see that it not only predicts the Lord's Passion and Death, but His victory over death, which the psalmist says shall be proclaimed by all believers because His death delivered us, His children, from ETERNAL death!

- As I meditate on the Passion and Death of Jesus, I see that He was willing to suffer and die a horrendous death for me. So now I must ask myself: What am I willing to do for Jesus?

- Take a step back. How is God preparing my loved one for his or her ultimate good – heaven – and how is He preparing me for life after my loved one is gone?

PRAYER:

Father, please help us to remember that You loved us so much that You sent Your only Son down to earth to suffer and die in order to redeem us. Jesus never gave up. He fought until the end. Help us to remember that we can do the same if, and only if, we walk the Way of the Cross hand in hand with Your Divine Son. Through the intercession of Jesus on the Cross, we ask You to send down the Holy Spirit upon us. Even as we feel the pain of this trial, help us to learn the lessons You wish to teach us. Most importantly, help us to keep our eyes fixed on You, our final destination. Amen.

Our Lady of Mount Carmel, Refuge in Affliction, pray for us.

Chapter 20

The Final Hospitalization/Hospice

*"Even though I walk through the valley of the shadow of death,
I fear no evil; for thou art with me;
thy rod and thy staff, they comfort me."
- Psalm 23:4 (RSVCE)*

A corner was turned the night that Stu was no longer able to keep anything down – not even water. He began to vomit the bile in his stomach. His skin was literally gray. I knew I was losing him.

I called an ambulance.

The paramedics placed my husband on a gurney in a sitting position and began to wheel him out to the ambulance. I was standing in the driveway and as they lifted him into the ambulance. Stu's eyes caught mine in a long, heart-wrenching, "S*o, it has come to this*" look. He knew, I knew: we were coming to the end of the road.

I am fortunate that Stu had great presence of mind until almost the very end of his life because when the ambulance driver asked to which of the many Birmingham area hospitals he should be taken, I started to request the local Catholic hospital. That's one thing we had agreed upon should it ever come to this.

However, Stu asked for a different hospital. When I looked at him questioningly, he said: "Because they did all those x-rays and tests just last week." Of course. That way a different hospital system wouldn't have to do the same tests all over again.

I followed the ambulance to the hospital. Something had to be done because my husband kept vomiting. A doctor came into the room and told us that Stu had to have a tube put up his nose and down into his stomach. I asked if there was any alternative. She said no. If we didn't do this, he would continue to vomit. That meant we had no choice.

I said to her, "This is important. My husband has a deviated septum, so he can only breathe out of one side of his nose. Please put the tube on the other side." She agreed.

I moved to the side of the room. She told me I had to leave. As a hardened veteran of the hospital system, I had no intention of leaving. I moved to the farthest corner of the room.

As I watched, a team converged around Stu's bed and the doctor immediately began to put the tube up the wrong side of Stu's nose! Because I was there, I was able to call out loudly: "Wrong side! Wrong side!"

Caregivers are absolutely vital to a patient's care. I was no longer surprised by this kind of thing, just grateful that God had given me the wisdom and the fortitude not to leave.

Lesson Learned: Stay in the room while in-room "procedures" like this are being done. It is unfortunate, but you can't be certain that doctors really "hear" you. They may just be agreeing so you'll let them get on with what whatever it is they feel must be done.

Stu was finally stabilized. Late that night, I left to get a few hours of sleep. When I arrived the next morning, Stu had already seen another doctor, who had shown him a set of x-rays. He told me that those x-rays showed that the cancer had eaten away part of his stomach.

I must have looked horrified at the news – or maybe it's just that my husband was very good at telling what I was thinking even when I didn't say anything. His sigh was full of an almost unbearable weariness. He looked at me and said: "Honey, if you want me to have one more operation…"

So much love! If I had said yes, he would have had that operation for me! But that was NOT what I was wanted. I was in anguish, but I didn't want him to die on the operating table with an operation that might kill him or, if we were lucky, extend his life for a week or two.

"No, honey, no. That's not what I want. It's okay. I understand."

As we were talking, another doctor entered the room. He took one look at Stu with the tube up his nose and said, "That has to be pretty uncomfortable. We can do a quick procedure so when you drink what comes down into your stomach will flow out into the tube in your stomach and you won't have to have a tube in your nose."

Stu immediately agreed.

Lesson Learned: Even in extreme circumstances, if something doesn't sound right, ask that another doctor be called into the room for a second opinion. Why did that first doctor tell us that a tube up Stu's nose was our only choice? I'll leave that to you to decide.

Lesson Learned: The Catholic Church teaches that food and water – basic nutrition – must NEVER be denied to a patient. But the Church does not require endless surgeries, experimental medicines or other extraordinary measures.

The doctors told me that Stu should soon be able to go home on hospice. Two different organizations quickly showed up for my consideration. I will talk about choosing a hospice in a moment. For now, I will just say that making a choice like this in an emergency is obviously not the best way to go.

In his final days in the hospital, Stu's heart began racing. He started to gasp and pant loudly, as if he had just run 100 miles in the desert heat without stopping. I was in Stu's room and there were so many doctors and nurses and aides in there, I was feeling overwhelmed. The doctor, who had made Stu more comfortable by taking the tube out of his nose, came over to me and said, "Come out to the hall with me."

As we stepped outside the room, he said, "Have you been through this before?"

I shook my head. He said, "Well, I have. Your husband is going to continue to have these heart incidents. They won't kill him, but he will wish he was dead. I'm going to have the patient advocate tell your insurance company that if they won't authorize you to have the medicine you need to give him to stop this, I won't allow him to go home. It will be much more expensive for him to stay in this hospital. You'll get it."

What a godsend that man was. Stu was eventually allowed to go home with the medicine which was, as the doctor had predicted, very much needed.

> **Lesson Learned:** Understand that exceptions can almost always be made. It's more expensive for a patient to remain in the hospital than to go on hospice. If your loved one needs something that isn't allowed on hospice, try to find a sympathetic doctor like this one who will help you get what you need. They're there!

Choosing a Hospice Provider

When my husband became a quadriplegic, I had to have help in order to keep him at home – so I had become familiar with home healthcare services. One of the aides with whom we had grown comfortable saw that I was interviewing hospice representatives. He asked why I didn't just use the hospice side of his company. He said he could make that happen with one phone call, and, because we were already in the company's system, it could happen immediately. That made sense, so I agreed.

Another mistake.

One of the hospice providers I had interviewed told me that her company was located near us. She said this would be an advantage. The home healthcare provider we had been using was headquartered across town. I asked if this would be a problem, but they assured me it wouldn't be because they had nurses who lived in our area. This would turn out to be a lie.

Lesson Learned: Whether the hospice provides in-home care or care in a hospice facility, choose a hospice provider who is located as close to your home as possible.

When hospice initially comes into your home, it becomes a whirlwind of activity. The bedroom quickly begins to look like a hospital room. You get a hospital bed, sheets, all sorts of equipment, including (in our case) IVs, and a ton of drugs for which you get myriad instructions.

Unfortunately, we did not get the heart medicine as quickly as we needed because Stu had another incident the day after he got home. It was a Sunday.

I immediately called hospice who said they would send someone right over. Two hours later, the nurse arrived. Two hours! Two hours of my husband gasping, heaving for breath, and wishing he would die. Two hours of my being unable to do anything to help him.

The nurse waltzed in wearing her Sunday finest. She had obviously been to church. She cheerfully administered the medicine he needed and left.

I was beside myself. I called the hospice to register a complaint. Even as a battle-hardened veteran, I thought the hospice administrator would be as upset as I was that their healthcare worker had taken two hours to get to our house, leaving their patient (my husband) in acute distress.

Instead, the woman said in a slow, even voice: "I *thought* you understood. This is end-of-life care. If you don't like it, perhaps you'd prefer to go with another provider."

Let that sink in. In other words, we know your loved one is dying, so, whatever is happening, we don't need to rush over. It doesn't matter if he is in distress. He's going to die anyway.

In normal circumstances, I would have had those people out of my home in a New York minute. But my husband, a quadriplegic, was dying. I couldn't have him moved out of his bed and put in the middle of a bunch of chaos as all of that equipment was switched out – something that heartless woman obviously knew.

There are so many great stories about hospice care and wonderful hospice nurses who do a yeoman's job caring for the dying. And to be fair, some of the other nurses who visited us were very caring.

Unfortunately, as my experience demonstrates, not every hospice company lives up to its marketing hype. This is an important decision. Choose carefully.

Lesson Learned: If I were faced with this again, I would, if possible, ask friends and a local priest or nun for hospice recommendations before I needed them. I would look at online reviews. If possible, I would choose a faith-based organization that saw hospice as a ministry, which it obviously is, and not just as a way to make money.

Lesson Learned: But what if your loved one dies, and you haven't forgiven each other? Thank God, all is not lost! I was blessed to have an interview with Father Paul Denizot of the Shrine of Our Lady of Montligeon in France, a world center of prayer for the Holy Souls in Purgatory. Because we, as Catholics, know and believe that we can pray for and to our loved ones after death, just as they can pray for us, Father says it is never too late to ask for forgiveness or to thank our loved one for something they did for us in this life. The Shrine even has a form visitors to the Shrine or to the Shrine's website can fill out to do just that. These forms are placed under the famous statue of Our Lady of Montligeon. (See Resources section for details.) But note, you can do the same thing at home!

REFLECTION QUESTIONS:

- What online research have I done, and what family, friends, doctors, priests, or co-workers have I spoken with about this, so I know what to do if the need for hospice arises?

- What people has the Lord sent me to help me make these decisions?

Prayer:

Jesus, one of the last words You said from the Cross is: "Father, forgive them, for they know not what they do" (Luke 23:34) (RSVCE). Please help us to forgive those who abandon us – as they abandoned you – in this hour of need. Instead of focusing on those who fail us, help us to put our focus on the doctors and nurses who help people like me navigate the system so my loved one gets the care he [or she] needs. Please bring me the doctor (or the hospice company) I need in this hour to help me bring my loved one home to You in the best possible way. Amen.

**Our Lady of Mount Carmel, Our Light in Darkness,
pray for us.**

Chapter 21

Making the Most of Your Final Days

"And Jesus said, "Father, forgive them;
for they know not what they do."
- Luke 23:34

My husband was only expected to live a week, maybe two. Instead, he lived for over a month, which was another great blessing.

Stu was loved by many people. During that month, I typed emails from him to friends from the Naval Academy, friends from our old neighborhood, and to the principal, fellow teachers, and students at his old high school, in particular one student who he knew would be especially distressed by his death.

The Blessings of Good Company

In Stu's final month, I was also blessed to have a home filled with the best people in the world.

My then 88-year-old Mom, who had just had an operation herself, and my immune-compromised younger sister who helped care for my Mom, could not make the trip to Alabama from Alexandria, Virginia.

But my beloved sister Marian came down to help. Marian put aside her own life for over a month to be with me. I will be forever grateful to her for that. While growing up, she had wanted to be a nurse, and, in these days, it became clear she would have been a good one.

When Stu had more of those rapidly beating heart incidents and we had to fill a syringe with medicine and slowly put it into the tube going into his body, Marian's steady hands were a Godsend. Little did either of us know that six years later, she too would die of cancer. My sister's husband and one of her grown children also flew down for a day or two.

My brother took time away from his busy job to join me at various times throughout Stu's illness. He paid for the care that allowed me to keep my husband home once he became a quadriplegic, and he would arrange for military honors at my husband's funeral. He would also take me with him on his family vacation after Stu's death, when I didn't know what to do with myself.

We also had the unbelievable blessing of having a priest friend from Pennsylvania join us, a priest whose own major health challenges made him the perfect support in such a crisis. Father Paul Stenson celebrated daily Mass in our home, which meant we could receive the Eucharist every day! Stu got just the tiniest sliver of the host or a drop of the Precious Blood, but that's all he needed. He could also go to Confession and receive the Anointing of the Sick. That is an incomparable blessing, for which I will never be able to thank this special priest enough.

Another beloved priest from our parish, who had given Stu Last Rites after a number of operations, also came by to hear my husband's Confession.

Because I worked at EWTN, we were blessed to have priests such as Fr. Joseph, Fr. John Paul, and Fr. Mark visit the hospital and our home on a number of occasions. Each priest imparted his own special blessing. It was from Fr. Joseph that I learned about the Apostolic Blessing. That blessing not only forgives sin,

BUT THE TEMPORAL PUNISHMENT DUE TO SIN. As I said in my previous Chapter, Author Susan Tassone, also known as the Purgatory Lady, calls the Apostolic Blessing the "deluxe package" to heaven!

Lesson Learned: All priests can give an Apostolic Blessing, but for some reason most do not think of it. So be sure to ask for this blessing. In fact, Susan Tassone suggests you put this in your will.

Stu's parents were both dead, and he only had one sister.

Stu did not want relatives we never saw to suddenly descend upon our house. That's an individual decision. What is important, however, is to let everyone you love fully understand that this is the end.

Stu's sister was uncertain about when to come down from her home in Arlington, Va. She could only take so much time away from her job. She asked if this really was the end, or should she wait a few more weeks? In other words, should she come before or after her brother's death?

I remember saying to her, "Dana, if you want to see your brother alive, come now. As my mother always says, 'You live for the living and not for the dead.'"

She came and both brother and sister benefited.

You may have to invite a family member to spend some time alone with your loved one. That's what I did after Dana arrived. She is very considerate, and I knew she wouldn't want to intrude.

Brother and sister spent at least an hour together. Later, I said to Stu: "Did you have a good conversation with your sister?"

He said, "Yes, I asked her to forgive me for everything I did to her growing up."

I nodded and said, "And did she ask you to forgive her for the things she did?"

He said, "No, but that's okay." And I could see it truly was.

Forgiveness

Before Stu died, I had the privilege of watching him forgive his father, with whom he had a fractious relationship; and six years later, I watched my sister completely forgive someone who hurt her and her family in a way that many would consider unforgiveable. This matters because we can't get to heaven carrying a load of unforgiveness in our hearts – no matter how justified it is.

But how? How can you do this? I want to share with you now something I learned after Stu died, which I think can also be applied to the whole problem of unforgiveness.

When I was going through Stu's cancers, amputation, and paralysis, I didn't have a lot of time to process what was happening. I had to be strong. But after Stu died, those memories came back to me with a vengeance. So many times I'd be driving to work and I'd remember something painful and I'd want to curl up in a ball and just weep. So I'd do something – anything – to distract myself from the memories.

But then, one day, I cried out: "Stop!" And I turned to the Lord in my heart and said: "Jesus, I don't want you to take away these memories because they are mine, and I want them. But I *need* You to take away the pain associated with this memory." And one by one, I lifted them up to my Savior, and one by one, He literally lifted the pain from my heart.

If He can do this with memories of a departed loved one, he can do it our feelings of unforgiveness, anger, or resentment. Whatever it is that you feel you can't forgive, give it to the Lord – one memory at a time – and allow Him to heal you.

I found out later that this is actually a spiritual "thing," but I didn't know that at the time. I just knew I needed help, and, having experienced His help throughout Stu's illness, I knew I could count on Him to help me afterwards.

You also might want to do what my widow friend Ellen did when her own husband was dying. She said the two of them not only verbally forgave each other for anything they had ever done to hurt each other, but they wrote it down and signed it. That way, she said, if she ever had any doubts, she could go back and look at that piece of paper and know that this was true.

Whatever is holding you or your spouse back from forgiving from your heart, give it to God. After all, we want our spouses to go to heaven, and we want to join then there when it's our turn to die. Don't let anything delay that blessed reunion!

Lesson Learned: Whatever it is you can't forgive – give it the Lord, ask Him to take away the pain associated with that memory, and He will help you.

Lesson Learned: If you or your loved one carry unforgiveness in your hearts, take the time to forgive each other. Then, consider writing it down and signing it. That way, if you later feel bad about something you said or did to your loved one, you can look at that piece of paper and know that you have been forgiven.

Lesson Learned: Remember, one of the blessings of a long illness is that it not only gives you the opportunity to say goodbye, but it also gives you the opportunity to get it right! Don't miss the opportunity!

REFLECTION QUESTIONS:

- Who does my loved one need to forgive before he or she dies? What can I do to facilitate a reconciliation?

- Have my loved one and I forgiven each other for ways we may have hurt each other during our lifetimes? If not, how can I now help to make that right?

PRAYER:

Dear God, as I stand beneath the Cross, help me to remember that my loved one's death is not just going to affect me. It may affect parents and siblings, cousins and co-workers, friends, neighbors, and students. As the caregiver, help me to reach out to others and to bring those most affected into my home or hospice so that they too may say their goodbyes; so that they too may forgive and be forgiven; so that they too may benefit from the freedom that comes from making things right before a loved one goes home. May our lives be a blessing to all who cross our paths at this time. Amen

**Queen of Heaven,
pray for us.**

STATION OF THE CROSS:
Jesus Dies on the Cross

"Father, into your hands I commend my spirit." Jesus' final words on the Cross. The moment for which we have been both fighting to avoid and preparing for is here. Caregivers: You are never going to be emotionally prepared for this. But if you have been following the advice in this book, your loved one is spiritually prepared to go home. Hang on to this. It will be of great comfort to you in your sorrow. Jesus' death opened the gates of heaven. Your loved one is now prepared to step through them!

Chapter 22

Final Moments: We Are Not Alone

"Father, into thy Hands, I commit my spirit!"
- Luke 23:46 (RSVCE)

As we got near the end of the road, I was in the bedroom with my husband when he said something that made me think he was losing his vision. I started to say something about that: "Maybe..."

He knew what I was about to say! "Don't say it! Don't say it," he cried. "I'm barely hanging on here."

I left the room and went to the altar in my prayer room. Among other things, it has a picture of Jesus that I just love.

I picked it up, looked at my Lord and said, "How am I supposed to do this? How am I supposed to watch my husband die?"

I took a minute to collect myself and then said through my tears: "Jesus, it's obviously not Your will that my husband live, so ... I'm giving him to You. But...but...and this HAS to be Your will...in return, I am asking that You turn his heart completely to You so that he can receive the highest degree of glory possible."

That may have been the best prayer I ever said for Stu. That's because my husband, who I believe was struggling to accept what was happening, suddenly couldn't get enough of the Sacraments! (If that's not what you meant, forgive me, my love.)

The grace was literally poured out immediately! I went into Stu's room and Father Paul was there. He said, "Stu, would you like to have Mass now?"

And I watched Stu turn a radiant face to him (I mean that, radiant) and breathe out one word with great reverence: "Yes!"

I watched as he participated with rapt attention in that Mass and later in a Rosary and a Divine Mercy Chaplet. God answers prayers. Maybe not always the way we want, but He hears the ones we really need. That is a hard memory to recount, but a beautiful memory.

It really was a time filled with God's blessings. All the people in my house were a blessing, but there were also signs that we weren't the only ones in the room.

At one point, I had made Stu comfortable in his bed. As I turned to leave the room Stu made a comment, which made me turn around and look at him. For several minutes, I didn't see Stu in that bed, but my father, who had died 23 years earlier. I blinked and my dad remained the whole time Stu was talking. I don't know that I even heard what Stu said. Gradually, Stu became visible to me again. We are not alone.

At another point, my sister and I were standing on either side of Stu's bed when my husband looked intently at the doorway and said: "Do you see that?"

My sister and I looked at each other, puzzled. "See what, honey?"

Stu smiled and suddenly started whistling as he rolled his eyes away from the doorway. Could it have been the angel of death? Could Stu have been whistling because he wasn't yet ready to go? As I said, during such times, we are not alone.

That would also be true for my sister, who would die of endometrial cancer several years later. She had been in immense pain before she lapsed into a coma. At one point, my brother was in the room with her, praying, when she opened her eyes and said to him: "I'm never sad." And then she went back to "sleep." Wow.

My mother used to say how brave Stu was – and she was right. A braver man I have never known. I believed my mother said that because she heard from me how hard he was fighting, but until this point I didn't think he had much choice about taking the fight on. I was wrong. When Stu finally decided he had endured enough, he started to fail quickly.

This was a man who had once said to me: "I don't want to leave you alone in this terrible world." But now, little by little, I watched Stu detach from the things of this earth, something we are all called to do.

First, he told me we had too much "stuff." We should just get rid of it all.

Second, he detached from our dogs, about whom he was absolutely crazy.

And then, most painfully, I watched him detach from me. Every time I left the house to drive somewhere during our 35 years of marriage, Stu always said: "Be careful. Precious cargo." The day he stopped saying that, I knew it wouldn't be much longer.

As my husband grew weaker, it was harder for him to talk. He spoke slowly to the two priests, Fr. Joseph and Fr. John Paul, who were visiting at the time. He wanted to know if his father, who was not a churchgoing man and with whom Stu had always had a difficult relationship, would go to heaven. He was very concerned about it. Later, I would remember that and have 30 Gregorian Masses said for Stu's dad. (See Chapter 11 for more on the special graces of Gregorian Masses.)

As Stu declined, he spoke less and less, and slept more and more, until one day he slipped into a coma. My sister and I didn't know if he could still hear us, so we kept speaking to him as if he could, and we were careful to keep his pain medicine going.

During that time, a priest from the Shrine of Divine Mercy in Stockbridge, Massachusetts was visiting EWTN. He came by our home and said the Divine Mercy Chaplet with us. That was another blessing because the Lord told St. Faustina if anyone says that chaplet even once, He will meet them as the Merciful Savior and not the Just Judge.

I had prayed to the Lord that He would let me be by my husband's side when he passed.

One day, I woke up, and I knew. I just knew.

I went downstairs and said to my sister, "I can't know this, but I think Stu is going to die today."

She said, "I do, too."

"I also think he's going to die at 3 p.m."

She just looked at me acceptingly.

Why did I say that? First of all, it was July 16, the Feast of Our Lady of Mt. Carmel, and I am a secular Carmelite. Our Lady called me into that order, and now I believed she was blessing me with the knowledge that she would be taking care of my husband – and of me.

Second, my husband's favorite devotion was the Divine Mercy Chaplet. During the time he was rehabilitating at Lakeshore Hospital, he would swim laps while praying the Chaplet.

Fr. Paul said Mass that day about 2 p.m. He always gave a wonderful little homily as well. When Mass was over, Father and Marian left to clean the vessels. I was left alone in the room with my husband. I looked up at the clock. 2:55 p.m.

I walked over to the bed and held his precious hand, and I watched his chest rise and fall, rise and fall, until, at 3 p.m., he simply stopped breathing.

I stood there for a minute, a sacred minute, the minute when I believe Our Lord and Our Lady came to get my husband. I had asked the Lord if I could be by my husband's side when he died and He granted that request.

Thank you, Lord!

I know that the timing and my foreknowledge of the timing was meant to be a comfort to me at that hour. I also knew as soon as I started talking, things would change, so I remained silent for several additional minutes, the last precious minutes I would spend alone with my husband.

Finally, I got my voice and called out: "He's gone. Stu is gone."

REFLECTION QUESTIONS:

- What does my loved one need from me now? "Permission" to go home? A prayer asking that his or her heart be turned completely to God?

- What prayers should I be saying by my loved one's bedside? The Divine Mercy Chaplet? The Rosary?

- What blessed objects is my loved one wearing? A Miraculous Medal? A Scapular?

PRAYER:

Blessed Mother, you stood at the foot of the Cross and watched your Son, who had been tortured and abused, die. And just as Simeon predicted, a sword pierced your heart. So, you, above all, understand the sword that has now pierced my own heart. I need to feel your loving presence and that of your Divine Son Jesus now. I ask to feel it. As I walk through the valley of the shadow of death, please grant me the same grace that you received at the foot the Cross, the grace that enabled you to say "fiat," even as your heart was breaking. Amen.

**Our Lady of Mount Carmel,
Consolation at the Hour of Death,
pray for us.**

STATION OF THE CROSS:
Jesus is Taken Down from the Cross and Laid in the Tomb

During His life and His death, Jesus endured everything He asks many of us to endure. He was mocked and humiliated, suffered and died, and like our future selves, He was buried. We know that when Jesus died, his disciples were afraid, and they were weeping. Mary Magdalene went to the tomb to be near the body of her Lord. You are now faced with laying your loved one to rest, and you too will weep. But beloved, as I reminded you in the last chapter, if you have been following the advice in this book, you will know you have done your best, and, despite your inevitable mistakes, you will have no regrets. I promise that, too, will be of great comfort to you in the days to come.

Chapter 23

Funerals...and the Aftermath

"If we have died with Him, we shall also live with Him;
if we endure, we shall also reign with Him."
- 2 Timothy 2:11-12

Fr. Paul and my sister came into the room. Marian hugged me and then called hospice. When you sign up for hospice, you are asked various questions about things like whether you want your loved one cremated and where he or she will be buried.

I stood there with my husband until the people from the funeral home arrived. I stood there as they prepared his body and as the hospice workers quickly dismantled everything they had brought in. One minute the room was like a hospital with all sorts of necessary equipment. The next it was empty. None of that equipment was needed anymore.

As the funeral home people started to leave the bedroom with my husband's body, my sister tried to take me aside. "You don't need to watch this."

I knew she was being kind, but I shook her off. "I've been with him the entire time," I said, not taking my eyes off of my husband. "I will be with him now."

I walked outside with him, and I watched as they drove away.

Back inside, I sat on the couch with my sister. I was numb. Other funeral home people arrived, and I suddenly had a million decisions to make. I was more than a little grateful when they left to have my sister and Fr. Paul with me.

My sister died two years ago. I know I mercifully don't remember all that happened in the next hours. I do remember wishing that I had written my husband's obituary beforehand because I was in no condition to do it at that time. I did, of course, write something up, but I know I would have done a better job had I not waited.

Fortunately, Stu and I had planned the funeral service together. Stu picked the songs and asked that the service end with the Navy Hymn. My friend Ellen, whose husband had been in the Navy, said she wished she had chosen that hymn for her husband's funeral.

As it turned out, Stu had two funerals. The first was in Alabama. It was celebrated by Fr. Paul and concelebrated by the friars at EWTN. How blessed I was! Marian and my brother, Larry, came down, but it was mostly for colleagues from EWTN and friends from the community.

The second was held in Alexandria, Virginia, where most of my family lived at the time, and which was closer to teachers and students at the high school where Stu taught, to his buddies from his Naval Academy days, and to our Pennsylvania neighbors and friends.

Lesson Learned: Plan the funeral services ahead of time. Be creative. If you need to have two funerals, if you need to have a funeral and a celebration of life, have it. Do whatever helps you most at the time.

My brother had arranged for military honors graveside. Since I didn't know whether I would remain in Alabama after I retired (I am still working at EWTN as of this writing), my husband and I decided that he should be buried in Alexandria, Virginia, near my father, who died in 1989. As long as my mother is alive, I know I will always return to that area for holidays and other family events.

My own gravesite and that of my mother were also purchased right next to our husbands at the time of their respective deaths. When picking out a gravestone, you will have to decide what you want to say. I went through a lot of different options in my mind (such as honor, integrity, and valor) but I finally settled on a phrase that was special to Stu and me.

When we were engaged to be married, Stu had to go away for a few weeks. During that time, he sent me flowers with a card that read: "Our hearts still touch across the miles of emptiness between us." I had part of that phrase – "Our hearts still touch" – etched on the gravestone. That was a good decision!

After the Funeral

Before the first funeral, I got some advice that I truly needed. I did not know what I was going to do with myself. Johnnette Benkovic (now Williams) called me seemingly out of the blue (but undoubtedly at the behest of the Holy Spirit) and said: "Michelle, don't go right back to work." Those simple words were a saving grace.

As God would have it, my brother had arranged a vacation for his own family, which just happened to occur right after the second funeral. He and his wife asked me to come with them to West Virginia. It was a blessing because, at the time, they had two boisterous young children (now teens) who were an antidote to my sadness, emptiness, and shock.

I had gone 100 mph for a very long time, always trying to think one step ahead. Now, that was over.

Lesson Learned: If possible, don't immediately return to work. The two or three days most companies allot for a funeral are not enough. If you can, spend time with family or friends in another location. If this is impossible, take a mini-vacation over the weekend: get outside, take a drive to a place you've never been before, give yourself some time to just "be" outside of the place that is so loaded with memories.

Returning Home

My dogs were staying with a pet sitter, and I knew I would have their wonderful companionship when I returned to Alabama. Still, I dreaded going back to a house without my Stu. So, I called my previously mentioned friend Ellen, a widow of a number of years, and asked if she would meet me at the airport and spend the weekend with me. She agreed. I will always love her for that.

REFLECTION QUESTIONS:

Lesson Learned: If possible, have someone who has been through the same thing you have, meet you at your home when you return and stay with you for a few days. It will help ease your transition.

- Who might I ask to be with me during and immediately after my loved one's death?

- Where and with whom might I go for a short time to regroup after the funeral?

- If I have left my home – or if I am fearful of being alone – do I have a family member or friend who would be willing and able to spend time with me at my home when it is time to return or after everyone leaves to go back to their own lives?

PRAYER:

Father, in Jesus' name, I ask You to send down Your Spirit upon me. Now that the battle for my loved one's earthly life is over, help me to know that I am not alone. You, who have stood by my side for so many years, stand by me now and give me a strong sense of Your presence, both internally and externally, through the people You send my way. Help me to accept the fact that, although my loved one's journey is over, mine is not. You still have plans for me. Help me to be open to what they are. Blessed Mother, please wrap your mantle of protection around me, and bless me again today with the comfort that you received from St. John the Apostle when your Son, Jesus, died. In Jesus' name I pray. Amen.

**Our Lady, Star of the Sea,
pray for us.**

STATION OF THE CROSS:
Resurrection

Death did not have the last word over Jesus, who would rise three days later. Neither does it have the last word over those of us who believe. If we have walked with Christ, there is a better life waiting for us on the other side. For those of us left behind, there is still work to do. But now, in addition to Jesus and Mary and all the canonized saints, we have another helper close by our side: our loved one, who will be cheering us on every step of the way!

Chapter 24

The Secret: Was the Fight Worth it?

"I have fought the good fight, I have
finished the race, I have kept the faith."
- 2 Timothy 4:7 (RSVCE)

Having read our story, what do you think? Was the fight worth it? I know my answer. It was more than worth it. I believe this was the most important thing I have ever done.

If my husband and I hadn't worked together to save his life, we never would have had our faith, hope, and love tested and strengthened; had so many beautiful conversations; forged an even stronger union by fighting together against a common enemy; had our limits tested in so many ways; enjoyed so many wonderful vacations, especially the memorable experience at a dude ranch in Wyoming; understood so deeply what it means to love another person as Christ loves us; met so many good people who prayed over us and helped us; and so much more.

In the fight for euthanasia occurring around the world at this writing, those on the pro-euthanasia side often talk about the inconvenience and expense family members may endure if a patient lives. Let's set aside the callousness and the unbelievable selfishness of that response for a moment.

Let me tell you a terrible secret about losing a loved one.

My husband was ill for eight years, so I had plenty of time to "prepare" myself for his death; to grieve in advance as caregivers often do; to imagine what life would be life without him. But here's the unfortunate thing: No matter how much time you spend imaging your loved one's death, no matter how prepared you think you are, let me assure of one thing: Emotionally, you are never prepared.

That's because you and I truly cannot imagine the world without our loved ones in it – and if you force the death before God wills it – you will grieve all the more. Why? Because you will have cut off all the amazing things that would have happened on your journey before the final goodbye; good things that the Lord had planned for you and your loved one from the beginning of time.

If you had a fractured relationship with your loved one, you may think you will escape that fate. Think again. From conversations with those in a grief group I would attend, I know that whenever we lose someone who we know loves us, even if it was a very imperfect love, it is a much bigger loss than we realize while they are living.

When my husband died, I was numb. But one thing was clear to me even then – and I remember saying it out loud to my sister and to Fr. Paul, who were with me at the time – "I have no regrets."

Oh, I know there are times, as I have recounted in this book, when I could have done something better. I made mistakes. God knows, I'm human and therefore not perfect. However, I do know that I did my best. And now that the war is over, and the battlefield is quiet – at least at the present moment – that knowledge sustains me.

When you've done your best, the Lord gives you the comfort of knowing in your heart that you have fought the good fight, that you have won the race, and I promise you, as hard as it will be without your loved one, the Lord will be with you in your brokenness.

I now know, with every fiber of my being, that I can depend on God in any future battle and in any future war – and I pray that you now know this is entirely possible for you too. You just have to ask.

This knowledge helped me to face the next big battle – Life After Stu – just as your battle as a caregiver will help you. I will write about picking up the pieces in my next book.

Until then, please remember: You and I can do all things through Christ who strengthens us. I hope to see you someday on "the other side."

Can I get an "Amen"?

Epilogue

Freely You Have Received; Freely Give

"But you are a chosen race, a royal priesthood, a holy nation,
God's own people, that you may declare the wonderful deeds
of him who called you out of darkness
into his marvelous light."
- 1 Peter 2:9 (RSVCE)

This was a hard book to write. It took me almost eight years. Over time, some dates became fuzzy, but the events themselves never are. When I counsel others who are going through similar events, I find that these memories come back strongly, and the Lord helps me remember the things I learned that might be helpful in the emergency this person is facing – and I am grateful that I have something to contribute.

You can't help if you don't know, and you won't know unless you go through it yourself. I am now able to say, like that wonderful doctor I mentioned in these final chapters, who said, "Have you been through this before? Well, I have, and let me tell you…"

For example, a woman from my Carmelite group had a stroke, and when she was ready for rehab, her daughter sent an email to our group asking for nursing home recommendations. I started to answer, and then I stopped. I remembered. Nursing homes don't provide the kind of rehabilitation a stroke patient needs. She needed to go to a hospital that specializes in rehabilitation or that has a rehabilitation wing. I wouldn't have known this if I hadn't been through this myself.

I called her daughter. She said one of the two hospitals in our area that had such a specialty had turned her mother down. The other had just visited. However, the daughter said she was reading some bad reviews online. I was able to tell her that while the hospital may not be perfect, they do a great job at their core mission of rehabilitating patients. Go! She did, and my friend did well.

Later, she transitioned to a nursing home where she was walked around a few times a day. She immediately realized for herself that there was no comparison. One day, you will find yourself able to make similar recommendations.

Our journey to Calvary has also made me more sensitive to others' pain, even in small ways. For example, my husband never put the kneeler down at church until the last minute because it was hard on his knees. One Sunday, I found myself in a pew with a woman who I could see had knee problems. The kneeler was up. When it came time for the consecration, the woman started to bend over to pull the kneeler down. I stopped her. "It's okay." She looked up gratefully. "Are you sure?" I nodded.

Before my experience with Stu, I probably wouldn't have noticed that she was in pain. Do I always see pain? No, but I know I'm *more likely* to see it now than I was before Stu and I went through so much together – and I'm grateful.

I was able to very gently suggest to another friend, who had slipped into a parental role with her very ill husband and was obviously getting frustrated about it, to consider going home and snuggling with him; to spend some time being his wife, instead of his parent.

When faced with a medical problem, I now know that I should search for available medical technology because someone else has undoubtedly faced the same problem. I know how to make a bed with a patient in it. I encourage friends to go on a vacation with a loved one even when things aren't perfect, and I frequently tell others who are grieving that they can still do something important, which is to have Gregorian Masses said after their loved ones dies (see Chapter 14 for details).

And I share so much more.

And you will, too. It's not knowledge we would ever have sought, but it is a gift that you and I were given as a result of our loved one's illness and/or death.

> *"You received without pay; give without pay."*
> -Matthew 10:8 (RSVCE)

Help others who are on their way to Eternal Life, and you will amass friends in heaven. Help other caregivers, and you will amass friends on earth. And hopefully, in the blink of an eye, which is what earthly life is compared to Eternity, all of us will one day meet our Creator, and He will be able to say to us, and to our loved ones:

"Well done, good and faithful servant; you have been faithful over a little, I will set you over much; enter into the joy of your Master"
-Matthew 25:21 (RSVCE).

One day, I also hope to meet you, dear readers, on the other side where *"He will wipe away every tear from [our] eyes, and death shall be no more, neither shall there be mourning nor crying nor pain any more..."* Rev 21:4 (RSV).

**God bless you,
fellow Soldiers in Christ!**

Appendix

Thirteen Saints to Walk with in Hard Times

The Church Triumphant provides us with many saints to whom we can pray. Here are a few I think are particularly relevant to caregivers:

1. *St. Teresa Benedicta of the Cross*
(Patron Saint of Martyrs/Loss of Parents)

In his homily during the canonization of Teresa Benedicta of the Cross (aka Edith Stein), Pope John Paul II quoted the new saint's words: "Whoever truly loves does not stop at the prospect of suffering. He accepts communion in suffering with the one he loves." Later he quoted her again, saying, "Love makes suffering fruitful, and suffering deepens love."

This Carmelite nun was born Jewish, and, after years of pretty much rejecting religion, converted to Catholicism. During World War II, she could have escaped the Nazis, but she remained in her convent where she was seized by the Gestapo, then shipped to Auschwitz, where she was murdered with her sister in a gas chamber. However, while in the concentration camp, Edith Stein was known for her compassion and caring for the other prisoners.

Caregivers, we have a choice. We can either enter into the suffering with our loved ones, giving them the love and care they deserve, or we can abandon them or treat them with hostility and grudging care. It's not always easy to be loving, but it's what we are called to do. Let us pray to this saint so that our loved ones may commend us for our compassion and caring just as Teresa's fellow prisoners commended her.

> **Suggested Reading:**
> Scaperlanda, Maria Ruiz. *Edith Stein: The Life and Legacy of St. Teresa Benedicta of the Cross.* Manchester, New Hampshire, Sophia Institute Press, 2017.
>
> To find the homily referenced above, search for Oct. 11, 1998, "Homily of John Paul II for the Canonization of Edith Stein."

2. *Pope Saint John Paul II*
(Patron Saint of the Family and of World Youth Day):

Pope John Paul II was probably best known for the words he spoke when he was elected Pope, and which he repeated throughout his pontificate: "Be Not Afraid." During his pontificate, the Pope faced many challenges: He celebrated Mass for the people of Poland under the watchful eyes of Communist soldiers, and is credited, along with President Reagan, with bringing down the Berlin Wall in a peaceful, nonviolent way. He not only showed physical courage in facing down Communist dictators, but spiritual courage after he was shot, and after his physical body began to decline precipitously.

"Be Not Afraid" is a great motto for caregivers as well. Our challenge is to stand up to our loved one's illness, to fight for them when fighting is needed, and to simply love them when loving is needed. Pope John Paul II is a good person to pray to when we are having a hard time doing this.

> **Suggested Reading:**
> Paul II, Saint John. *In God's Hands: The Spiritual Diaries of Pope John Paul II,* San Francisco, Harper One, 2017.

3. *Our Lady of the Miraculous Medal (aka Our Lady of Grace)*

I owe my devotion to Our Lady, especially under this title, to my mother. During the 1800s, Our Lady appeared to Sister Catherine Laboure (now a saint), who was a novice with the Daughters of Charity in Paris. During the second of two apparitions, Our Lady appeared to this budding saint in the image of a medal that she wanted to be made available to the whole world. She said those who wear it, especially around the neck, will receive great graces.

The medal shows rays streaming from rings on Our Lady's hands. These rays represented the graces that people have requested from Our Lady. But during the apparition, Sister noticed that some of the gems were dark. These represent graces that have not been requested. The medal also contains a prayer: "O Mary, conceived without sin, pray for us who have recourse to thee." Reciting this prayer with devotion places you under the protection of the Mother of God – something both caregivers and patients will appreciate.

One of the prayers of the Miraculous Medal Novena is the powerful *Memorare*, which my mother requested that I say before going on a date while in college. (Smart Mom!) I know that wearing it kept me safe then – just as it does now.

Suggested Readings:

Two U.S. Shrines, with corresponding associations, honor Our Lady of the Miraculous Medal. *Both Shrines are open to the public.*

You can find the Novena to Our Lady of the Miraculous Medal, which includes the powerful *Memorare* prayer, on the website of The Central Association of the Miraculous Medal (CAMM) in Philadelphia, Pennsylvania. CAMM also offers up to 500 free Miraculous Medals upon request. http://www.miraculousmedal.org/

Read the story of the Miraculous Medal on the website for The Association of Our Lady of the Miraculous Medal in Perryville, Missouri. Their grounds feature a gorgeous Rosary Walk in addition to the Shrine.

---

4. *St. Teresa of Calcutta*
(Patron Saint of the Missionaries of Charity, World Youth Day, and the Archdiocese of Calcutta)

Mother Teresa was a modern day Veronica. She was, without a doubt, the 20th Century's best known and loved caregiver!

What was her secret? After her death, Angelo Comastri, Archbishop of Loreto, wrote a beautiful piece on Mother in which he recalled asking her this same question. But instead of answering, she shocked him by asking the Archbishop how many hours he spent in prayer each day. He was offended, and told her he had expected to speak with her about how to help the poor, not to be grilled about his prayer life! But he says she grabbed his hands and said: "My child, without God, we are too poor to be able to help the poor! Remember: I am only a poor woman who prays. When I pray, God puts His Love into my heart, and so I can love the poor. By praying!"

I remember telling my sister that Mother Teresa's sisters spend 3 ½ hours in prayer *every day*. (That includes Mass, Adoration, spiritual reading, mediation, and night prayers.) We were both surprised. But as Archbishop Comastri's conversation shows, we shouldn't have been. Working with the "poorest of the poor" isn't an easy job. Neither is caregiving. We don't have to be on our knees all day, but if we're not praying, wherever we are, we will fall. Only in and with Christ are we up to the task – even if we are going through a dark night of the soul as Mother Teresa did. (see book below).

Suggested Readings:

Mother Teresa, Kolodiejchuk, Brian (Ed.). *Mother Teresa: Come Be My Light: The Private Writings of the Saint of Calcutta.* New York, Doubleday Religion, 2007.

To find the piece mentioned above, search for: "This Is How I Remember Her," by Angelo Comastri, Archbishop of Loreto and President of the National Committee for the Great Jubilee of the Year 2000."

5. *St. Padre Pio*
(Patron Saint of Civil Defense Volunteers, Adolescents, Stress-Relief, and Pietrelcina)

The great saint of Pietrelcina in Italy is perhaps best known for his admonition: "Pray, hope, and don't worry!" Padre Pio suffered great physical pain from his stigmata, which bled copiously, as well as great personal pain when he was forbidden to hear confessions, even though he had the gift of reading hearts. Despite all of this, he stayed close to the Lord, who rewarded him with many gifts such as the ability to bilocate, the gift of prophecy, the gift of healing, and much more. Padre Pio's life wasn't easy, but it was meaningful because he fulfilled the plan that God had for him.

Did Padre Pio ever question why he couldn't hear confession, or why he had the "gift" of the stigmata? If he did, he didn't let that stop him from doing whatever it was the Lord asked him to do. As caregivers, we, too, are called to fulfill the plan God has for us, even in the midst of trials and bodily afflictions. St. Pio, please help us to trust that the Lord's plans are always better than our own. Please read my soul, and help me to see where I can improve.

Suggested Reading:

Franciscan Friars of the Immaculate, Francis Mary (Ed.) *Padre Pio: The Wonder Worker.* San Francisco, CA., Ignatius Press, 1999.

---

6. *St. Peregrine*
(Patron Saint of Persons Suffering from Cancer, HIV/AIDS, or Other Illness)

No one would have guessed that Peregrine Laziosi, a rebellious young man who physically struck a priest, would become a saint. But when this former gang member was forgiven by the priest he attacked, Peregrine was so overwhelmed that he not only became a Catholic, but he also eventually became a Servite priest, who spent his life helping the sick, the poor, and the homeless. However, he is best remembered for having cancer of the leg. The night before his leg was to be amputated, Peregrine asked the crucified Lord to heal him. When he woke the next morning, he was cured.

This saint is obviously very popular with cancer patients, and with anyone suffering from a serious illness. He is also a good saint to pray to if your loved one is having a hard time forgiving someone. He knows the power of forgiveness since he himself was converted when he received mercy and not justice from the priest he attacked. St. Peregrine, please intercede for us so that our loved one may be healed in body and in spirit if it be the will of God.

Suggested Reading:

Search for and pray the well-known Novena and/or the Prayer to St. Peregrine.

---

7. *St. Thérèse of the Child Jesus and the Holy Face*
(Patron Saint of the Sick)

In her autobiography, *Story of a Soul,* St. Thérèse of Lisieux talks about caring for an aged nun who was always complaining. One day, as she was wheeling the nun in her wheelchair, this little saint had a vision of a ballroom. Men and women were whirling about the dance floor dressed in their finest clothes. But instead of feeling envious, St. Thérèse knew, in that moment, that there was nowhere else she'd rather be. And though the elderly nun sometimes tested her patience, Thérèse treated her with such kindness that her patient was heard telling the other nuns that she didn't know why St. Thérèse loved her so much. St. Thérèse is a good person to pray to when our patience is similarly tested by a complaining patient.

Suggested Reading:

Clark, John, O.C.D. (Trans.) *St. Therese of Lisieux: Her Last Conversations.* Washington, D.C., ICS Publications, 1977.

---

8. *St. Elizabeth of the Trinity*
(Patron Saint Against Illness, of Sick People, & of Loss of Parents)

This saint lived only five years as a Carmelite nun before succumbing to a painful death from Addison's disease. But in those years, she found her own little way, just as St. Therese found hers. She once wrote: "We must be mindful of how God is in us in the most intimate way and go about everything with him. Then life is never banal. Even in ordinary tasks, because you do not live for these things, you will go beyond them."

It seems like the Carmelite saints, who are known as masters of prayer in the Catholic Church, are intent on showing us that we must walk with God, talking to Him in the same way we talk to a trusted friend. This can make the ordinariness of every day – even when it involves helping our loved one with toileting – something extraordinary.

Dear St. Elizabeth of the Trinity, I'm having a hard time seeing this as extraordinary. Help me to see beyond what I am being called to do by keeping my mind focused on Our Lord. Amen.

Suggested Reading:
Elizabeth of the Trinity. *The Complete Works of Elizabeth of the Trinity, vol. 2 (featuring Her Letters from Carmel)*. Washington, D.C. ICS Publications, 1995.

---

9. *St. Faustina*
(Patron Saint of Mercy)

Jesus entrusted this young nun with the mission of bringing the Divine Mercy message and the Divine Mercy Chaplet to the world. She encountered numerous obstacles along the way, including her own poor health. At one point, Jesus asked Sister Faustina to do something for Him that required her to be in good health. For the first time in years, she became healthy. However, after completing her task, it occurred to Sister Faustina that she might be more pleasing to the Lord as a sick person, so she told Jesus that, if it was His will, He could make her sick again...and so He did.

The first time I read that, I remembered gasping out loud. Could I ever be so conformed to the Will of God that I would say such a thing? Not of myself! But when we strive to become other Christs, which is only possible by conforming ourselves to His Will, we are on the road to sanctity. Let us pray for the grace to love God as much as He loves us. Only then, like the nun we now call SAINT Faustina, will we be able to do whatever God wants, whenever He wants it.

Suggested Reading:
_____, *Diary of Saint Maria Faustina Kowalska*. Stockbridge, MA, Marian Press, 2019.

---

10. *St. Rita*
(Patron Saint of Widows, the Sick, Bodily Ills, Wounds, and Impossible Causes)

When her husband was killed by a rival, Rita's sons vowed revenge. Rita prayed that the Lord would take her sons rather than allow them to fall into mortal sin. She understood what really mattered. Jesus heard her prayer. Pray to St. Rita when you need help focusing on what matters most and, later, when you need to find hope in the face of a loved one's death.

Suggested Reading:
Sicardo, Fr. Joseph O.S.A. *St. Rita of Cascia: Saint of the Impossible (Wife, Mother, Widow, Nun)*. Charlotte, N.C., Tan Books, 1993.

---

11. *Brother Lawrence of the Resurrection*
(Known for His Deep Love of God in All Circumstances)

Lawrence was not a priest, but a brother, a deacon, and a martyr. He is renowned for writing *The Practice of the Presence of God*. This book is a classic that gives very simple, practice advice on how to find joy by keeping Christ in our thoughts, no matter what we are doing. Brother Lawrence found this joy despite the difficulties in his life, and he invites us to find it too. He says:

"[W]hen we begin our Christian walk, we must remember that we have been living in the world, subject to all sorts of miseries, accidents, and poor dispositions from within. The Lord will cleanse and humble us in order to make us more like Christ. As we go through this cleansing process, we will grow closer to God

"Therefore, we should rejoice in our difficulties, bearing them as long as the Lord wills, because only through such trials will our faith become purified, more precious than gold."
(see 1 Peter 1:7; 4:19.)

Suggested Reading:

Brother Lawrence of the Resurrection. *The Practice of the Presence of God.* Washington, D.C., ICS Publications, 1994. Maalouf, Jean.

Practicing the Presence of God: A Retreat with Brother Lawrence of the Resurrection. Washington, D.C., ICS Publications, 2011.

---

12. *St. Michael the Archangel*
(the Lead Angel in the Battle Against Satan, and the Archangel Who Assists Us at the Hour of Death)

13. *St. Joseph*
(Patron of a Happy Death)

No list of saints for caregivers is complete without St. Michael and St. Joseph! Statues of the Archangel Michael always depict him as a soldier with Satan beneath his feet. Among other things, St.

Michael is the Archangel who rescues us from Satan at the hour of death, if that is necessary, and who leads us to our judgment in heaven – so he's a good angel to have on our side. But so is the great St. Joseph. Lest we forget, he is well-known as the patron of a happy death, which means he helps assure that we die in a state of grace. St. Michael, the Archangel, defend us in battle! St. Joseph, pray for us now and at the hour of our death. Amen.

Mother Mary Angelica
(Foundress of Eternal Word Television Network)

While not a canonized saint, Mother Angelica is a great example of a woman who courageously accepted her cross and taught others to do the same.

The miraculous healing of Mother Angelica's leg is well known to EWTN's many viewers. They celebrated with her as the formerly crippled nun danced on television before a worldwide audience. But later in life, Mother suffered a cerebral hemorrhage. She traveled to Lourdes in the hope of a physical healing. This time, it was not to be.

However, in his biography on Mother Angelica, Author Raymond Arroyo says that Mother received something much more valuable than a physical healing while at Lourdes: a deeper understanding and acceptance of her cross. That makes her the ideal person to whom we can pray when our prayers are not answered the way we want them to be.

Suggested Readings:
_____, *Mother Angelica on Suffering and Burnout.* Irondale, Alabama, EWTN Publishing, Inc., 2016.

Arroyo, Raymond. *Mother Angelica: Her Grand Silence: The Last Years and Living Legacy,* New York City, Random House LLC, 2016.

Conclusion

Dear Caregiver, if you have walked the Way of the Cross with your seriously ill loved one, you now understand what it is like to be cleansed and humbled by Our Lord so that you might grow closer to Him. Your faith may have been weak, but having stretched out your hand to God, and having experienced His Hand in your own as you faltered, you now understand that your faith truly is more precious than gold. You now have a relationship with the Lord – one you may not have had at the beginning of this walk – and I promise you, that relationship will sustain you in the years to come.

"[T]here is no way to heaven except the way of the cross.
I followed it first. You must learn that
it is the shortest and surest way."

– Jesus to St. Faustina
Diary of St. Faustina, Entry 1487

Resources

How to Share Health Updates with Family and Friends:

If you don't want to keep repeating the same health update to everyone you know, sign up for a site like Caring Bridge, https://www.caringbridge.org/. This is an incredibly helpful site, where you or a loved one can post updates for the family and friends you allow to access your page.

Where to Have 30 Gregorian Masses Said:

The tradition of having 30 Gregorian Masses said for your deceased loved one is discussed more fully in Chapter 14. Here's where to go to have such Masses said:

- *Seraphic Mass Association,* 5217 Butler St., Ste. 100, Pittsburgh, PA 15201-2657, or go online to https://mymassrequest.org, click on Request a Mass at the top of the page, and then Gregorian Masses on the drop down menu.

- *Pious Union of St. Joseph for the Suffering and Dying,* 953 East Michigan Ave., Grass Lake, MI 49240, or go online to www.piousunionofstjoseph.org.

- *The National Shrine of Our Lady of Czestochowa,* 654 Ferry Road, Doylestown, PA 18901, or go online to place your order: https://czestochowa.us/gregorian-masses-request-form/

How to Say 'I'm Sorry' or 'Thank You' to a Loved One Who has Passed:

The Shrine of Our Lady of Montligeon in France has been designated as a world center of prayer for the Holy Souls in Purgatory. Because we, as Catholics, know and believe that we can pray for and to our loved ones after death, just as they can pray for us, Father Paul Denizot, Shrine Rector, says it is never too late to ask for forgiveness or to thank our loved one for something they did for us in this life. The Shrine even has a form on its website to do just that: https://montligeon.org/en/a-thank-you-sorry-card-to-a-deceased-person/. These forms are placed under the famous statue of Our Lady of Montligeon.

The Shrine also offers retreats for the bereaved and much more.

How to Say the Rosary:

Go to https://www.ewtn.com/catholicism/library/how-to-say-the-rosary-9153

How to Say the Chaplet of The Divine Mercy:

Go to https://www.ewtn.com/catholicism/devotions/chaplet-of-the-divine-mercy-387

Select On-Demand Movie and Television:

- **EWTN Global Catholic Network:** www.EWTN.com/ondemand

- **Pure Flix Films:** www.pureflix.com

Great Catholic CDs:

Look for albums by The Priests, the Dominican Sisters of Mary, and St. Paul's Choir School.

Selected DVDs:

- **Finding God in All Things:** Father Timothy Gallagher's bestselling EWTN television series, which teaches you how to find God in all things through St. Ignatius of Loyola's beautiful Examen Prayer: http://bit.ly/FindingGodInAllThings.

- **Living the Discerning Life:** Learn how to tell if you are experiencing spiritual consolation or spiritual desolation and what to do about it. Based on the teaching of St. Ignatius of Loyola. Find it here: http://bit.ly/LivingTheDiscerningLife.

Where to Get Help Making Moral Decisions About Healthcare

The National Catholic Bioethics Center in Broomall, Pennsylvania, is a treasure trove of information, www.ncbcenter.org. From that website, you can not only ask an NCBC ethicist for guidance in moral decision making, but, in emergency situations, you can even call 215-877-2660 anytime, day or night, and someone will help you.

Where to Get Financial Help

The U.S. Government's free Eldercare locator (https://eldercare.acl.gov) offers a boatload of state resources by city and state or by ZIP code. If your loved one is not elderly, they might still be able to help by referring you to appropriate resources.

Bibliography

In addition to the books recommended in the **Thirteen Saints To Walk with in Hard Times** section in the Appendix, the four books below were mentioned in the text of this book:

DeStefano, Anthony. *A Travel Guide to Heaven*. New York City. Image, Doubleday, 2005.

Frankl, Viktor. *Man's Search for Meaning*. Beacon Press, 1st edition, June 1, 2006.

Tassone, Susan. *Day By Day for the Holy Souls in Purgatory*. Huntington, IN. Our Sunday Visitor Publishing Division, 2014.

_____, *Spiritual Warfare Prayers*, Denver, Colorado, Valentine Publishing House.

Acknowledgements

No one writes a book alone. My first thanks must always go to my Lord and Savior Jesus Christ and to His Blessed Mother Mary, who were with me every step of this journey and without whom I could not think, say, or do anything of value. All glory to you, my Lord!

I also send my love and everlasting thanks to my incredible husband Stuart Johnson. This book is being published on the 10th anniversary of his death. I am most blessed among women to have had the love of such an incredible man.

I also owe so much of any good that is in me to my family, who support me in everything I do: To my wonderful Mom, who guided me through so much of my life and who now has dementia, I give thanks for teaching me the faith and for being such a wonderful example of faithfulness to God even in her current illness. I also give thanks to my now deceased sister Marian, who was so supportive through Stu's illness; to my sister Yvonne, who prayed me through so many emergencies; and to my brother Larry, whose love and support included paying for the home health aides I was able to hire after Stu became a quadriplegic.

Debbie Georgianni (from "Take 2 With Jerry & Debbie" on EWTN radio) and her husband, Marty, were the first to read the book (out loud and to each other during a vacation!) and to encourage me to get it out! If Debbie hadn't insisted on reading it and being so enthusiastic about it, I might still be dithering over it! I love you, my sister!

Thanks also to my dear friend, Susan Brinkmann, a prolific author who frequently appears on EWTN Radio's "Women of Grace" and who is the co-founder of "Live Catholic." Her many acts of friendship, which I reference in the book, were key as we made our way from Pennsylvania to Alabama while Stu was so ill. She generously shared her knowledge of publishing with me, answering endless questions, and sharing contacts who made the publishing process possible. Thank you, my sister!

One of the people Sue recommended was Beth Racine, editor extraordinaire, who went through the book with a fine-tooth comb finding all those little errors and asking great questions. The book is better for her help. Thank you, Beth!

I also want to thank the best graphic designer in the world, Christina M. Walsh. I hired her right out of college to work at the newspaper at which I was the editor. Her beautiful faith always led her to create inspired designs, so I asked her to design the cover for this book. She is the one who found the incredible image readers see on the cover. At first, we didn't know where it came from. Christina investigated and discovered that the image was created by Artist Joe Alblas for the television mini-series, "The Bible," starring Roma Downey as Mary. She and her husband Mark Burnett produced the series. May God bless them for the work they do for the Kingdom of God.

My heartfelt thanks to Roma Downey, who so incredibly and generously responded to my request to use the image on the cover, and to MGM, who gave us permission to use the image that so beautifully says graphically what the book says in words. I cannot thank them enough for the honor of using the image on the cover.

I also want to thank my friend Johnnette Benkovic Williams (Host of EWTN's "Women of Grace"), whom I reference in the book. Among other things, she's the person who advised me to take some time off after my husband's death rather than immediately returning to work, and her friendship in the years after Stu died was a real blessing in my life. May the Lord continue to bless you, my friend!

And many thanks to Colin Donovan, EWTN's Vice President of Theology and a theologian, who read the book and suggested a number of theological tweaks, which make me feel confident that everything in the book is solidly Catholic!

I also want to thank all those who took the time to read the book and to express their support for it. These include Raymond Arroyo (Host of EWTN's "The World Over with Raymond Arroyo"); Anthony DeStefano, bestselling author of over 20 Christian books for adults and children; Teresa Tomeo (a prolific author, host of EWTN Radio's "Catholic Connection," and co-host of "The Catholic View for Women); and Janet Morana (Executive Director of Priests for Life and an author herself). I am blessed to work with all of these people who make my world brighter for being in it!

I also want to thank bestselling author Susan Tassone for generously sharing her book publishing and marketing expertise with me. She is another good friend and advisor whom I am blessed to have in my life!

Finally, many thanks to EWTN President & COO Doug Keck (Host of "EWTN Bookmark," and co-host of "Father Spitzer's Universe"). He is a wonderful boss whose support for this book is allowing me to appear on EWTN television and radio, and for the book to be made available to the public via EWTN Religious Catalogue. God bless you, Doug!

✝

About the Author

Michelle Laque Johnson has more than 30 years of journalism and communications experience, and currently serves as Director of Communications for EWTN, the largest religious media network in the word. Under her leadership as Editor-in-Chief of *The Catholic Standard & Times*, the Philadelphia Press Association awarded the paper First Place for overall weekly coverage for the first time in its history. She is an award-winning editor and reporter, having worked for a metropolitan daily newspaper and several national publications, including *Investor's Business Daily*.

Michelle won two Gabriel Awards, one for a social media campaign and the other for the "Inside EWTN" blog she authors, and has received journalism awards for column writing, investigative reporting, business and economic news, and more. She is also a Secular Carmelite.

Michelle was especially honored to receive the Neumann Award from the Catholic Philopatrian Literary Institute for being "an exemplary Catholic woman who has made an outstanding contribution to family, church, profession, or country, and whose courage and integrity are unquestionable."

Let's Continue the Conversation:

Find out more about Michelle's new Caregivers of the Cross group on social media, get updates on her next book, learn when her new podcast is launching, and get even more information about caregiving at www.CaregiversOfTheCross.com.